Coaching and Trauma

Coaching in Practice series

The aim of this series is to help coaching professionals gain a broader understanding of the challenges and issues they face in coaching, enabling them to make the leap from being a 'good-enough' coach to an outstanding one. This series is an essential aid for both the novice coach eager to learn how to grow a coaching practice, and the more experienced coach looking for new knowledge and strategies. Combining theory with practice, the series provides a comprehensive guide to becoming successful in this rapidly expanding profession.

Published and forthcoming titles:

Bluckert: *Psychological Dimensions to Executive Coaching*

Bluckert: *Gestalt Coaching: Right Here, Right Now*

Brockbank and McGill: *Coaching with Empathy*

Brown and Brown: *Neuropsychology for Coaches: Understanding the Basics*

Driver: *Coaching Positively: Lessons for Coaches from Positive Psychology*

Hawkins: *Creating a Coaching Culture*

Hay: *Reflective Practice and Supervision for Coaches*

Hayes: *NLP Coaching*

McGregor: *Coaching Behind Bars: Facing Challenges and Creating Hope in a Women's Prison*

Paice: *New Coach: Reflections from a Learning Journey*

Pemberton: *Resilience: A Practical Guide for Coaches*

Rogers: *Building a Coaching Business*

Rogers: *Coaching for Careers: A Practical Guide for Coaches*

Sandler: *Executive Coaching: A Psychodynamic Approach*

Vaughan Smith: *Therapist into Coach*

Vaughan Smith: *Coaching and Trauma: Moving Beyond the Survival Self*

Wildflower: *The Hidden History of Coaching*

Coaching and Trauma

Moving Beyond the
Survival Self

Julia Vaughan Smith

Open University Press

Open University Press
McGraw-Hill Education
8th Floor, 338 Euston Road
London
England
NW1 3BH

First published 2019

Senior Commissioning Editor: Hannah Kenner
Head of Open University Publishing: Laura Pacey
Content Production Manager: Ali Davis
Editorial Assistant: Karen Harris

A catalogue record of this book is available from the British Library

ISBN-13: 9780335248421
ISBN-10: 033524842X
eISBN: 9780335248438

Library of Congress Cataloging-in-Publication Data
CIP data applied for

Typeset by Transforma Pvt. Ltd., Chennai, India
Printed and bound by CPI Group (UK) Ltd, Croydon, CR0 4YY

Praise for this book

"The elephant in the coaching room is so often the underlying trauma which is causing the client's stuckness. "Coaching and Trauma" *master-fully demonstrates how common coaching dilemmas - imposter syndrome, the inner critic, career derailment, burnout, bully/victim dynamics - can be traced back to trauma. It then shows how, with these insights, coaches can guide clients out of unhelpful survival strategies back towards healthy autonomy. This book busts the myth that trauma has nothing to do with coaching, while underlining clearly how coaches can maintain appropriate boundaries. A real gift to the profession and absolutely essential reading any coaching supervisor."*

Paul Heardman, Leadership Coach and Coaching Supervisor

"Necessary reading for anyone serious about coaching. It's a profound book, and because it goes deep, it reveals fertile possibilities. It touches, evokes and - with great care - honours our necessary inventiveness. What curious predicaments we get ourselves into! What strange patterns we recreate in our behaviours and relationships! Working environments are awash with opportunity for people to replay the victim, perpetrator or rescuer responses through which they first adapted to the world. So often, coaching succeeds when a client discovers that it might be possible to approach a work situation in a slightly different way, and this apparently minor adjustment opens the door to many other opportunities. Yet sadly, organisations are overwhelmingly traumatising for the people who work in them, and coaches can be confronted with clients close to the edge of their capacities. To recognise this, understand and appreciate the condition is the first great gift that a coach brings to his or her client. In this way coaching can make a tremendous contribution to responsible leadership - to which book provides crucial underpinnings.

Jonathan Gosling, Emeritus Professor of Leadership,
Exeter University and co-founder of CoachingOurselves.com

"This book should interest therapists and coaches. If not, they should ask themselves why. I highly recommend it to anybody who manages or spends time with people. It may also appeal to parents. I suggest you read the book through then return to graze selectively on the things that resonate

and don't get hung up on the bits that don't feel relevant. Don't expect to "get it" on the first read, there is a lot to digest.

Any manager reading this book can learn a great deal to make them a better manager and a better person. If you are at all reflective, this book should help in your understanding and dealing with people, particularly those with whom you have some difficulty relating. Once learned, you will never un-learn some of the ideas in this book. If you take nothing else away, take this: "Whenever tempted to rescue, other than saving a life, don't." (Bottom of Page 80, to save you looking).

Keep a copy of this book nearby because you will want to dip in and revisit some ideas and others will simply creep up on you."

"When I was reading Coaching and Trauma there were many occasions where I wanted to query, challenge, disagree or seek more knowledge because I was wholly engaged in the material. That means that it is good writing. Please read this book if you are a coach, therapist or manager and you want to be better at what you do. Read this book if you work with people and want to be better at that. But also read this book because you are a person and you will be better at who you are"

"This book is a magnificent fusion of Julia's career as a clinician, manager, management consultant, therapist, coach and author. It is built around the work of others but Julia brings her own special insight, flair and understanding of people to create a book that works on many levels. For the layperson there is a lot to trigger reflection of their own life and relationships. For all managers this book is an essential addition to your craft to help you be a better manager and person. For therapists and coaches this work adds to Julia's earlier publication Therapist into Coach and both books should be compulsory reading for all who practise in these fields."

"I read this book from a management perspective yet it is so much more. All the material will be of particular relevance to therapists and coaches but a great deal should also be of interest to managers and anybody else concerned with relating better to people. The style and structure enable the book to be used at many levels and each chapter can stand alone. In the examples and case studies managers will recognise much of their own experience in dealing with people issues and gain perspectives to better understand and manage them in future. Applying insights from this book should lead to more satisfied and productive people and workplaces."

Brian Lewis, Bellettes Bay Company,
Tasmania, Australia

"Jules' new book fills an important gap in the coaching market. She gives us an in-depth yet accessible outline of what trauma is and how it can play out in our coaching work.

The great advantage of this is that we can avoid the pitfalls of typical coaching over-reactions to client behaviour like rescuing, carrying their burdens, or feeling guilty if they don't seem to be getting anywhere. Jules shows how, very often, these 'default' responses are typical, uninformed reactions to a client's trauma. Indeed the client themselves may be unaware of their trauma still affecting them.

Jules shows how it is not our role to deal directly with these traumas (a great relief to me) but that a deeper awareness of them and our own potential reactions can help us ask the right questions, ensure the client retains ownership of their issues and enable us to look after ourselves too.

How do we do this? A powerful lesson here from Jules is that we coaches don't need more tools (that in itself is a challenge for many coaches) but we need to work more on ourselves. It's not about doing things to our clients, but about who we are.

This book is the latest in the coaching series edited by Jenny Rogers which continues to produce important and new insights for the coaching community."

Matt Driver, Matt Driver Consulting

"Julia Vaughan Smith writes about a hugely important subject, so often invisible, in a detailed and highly knowledgeable way. Her treatment of a complex and difficult subject is sensitive and skillful and is written in a clear and accessible style. This is an immediately practical book with a sophisticated framework for practice combined with wise guidance in what will always be a challenging area for most coaches. I thoroughly recommend this book to practicing coaches, supervisors, and coaches-in-training."

Peter Bluckert

"In this well-researched, practical and highly readable book, Julia Vaughan Smith explains how early trauma can impact us in our day-to-day lives and shows up in coaching. She describes the various ways that a client can present in coaching through their trauma, survival and healthy selves, she advises us to work with the client's healthy self and how to recognise if we are getting entangled with the client and what to do about it. The theory is brought to life with personal examples from Julia's own life story and relevant coaching case studies. Trauma and Coaching is essential reading for coaching supervisors and coaches and the important messages in the book can be shared, in an appropriate way, with clients. I thoroughly recommend it – it has transformed my practice."

Dr Louise Sheppard, Coaching Supervisor and
Executive Coach at Praesta Partners LLP

"*I am delighted to see this book being published. I enjoyed the journey Julia takes us on, bringing clarity to this complex subject. She balances theory plus practicality and keeps the focus firmly on coaching. I particularly value her examples, including her personal ones, alongside the practical questions and approaches. The book is a must for anyone wanting to take their coaching to another level. I do feel equipped now to incorporate, with care, this work into my coaching. Thank you.*"

Shirley Greenaway, Executive Coach,
Head of Coaching at Management Futures

"*This is a book that coaching has been missing. It is a valuable resource for any coach, supervisor or training provider interested in the development of a more mature coaching profession. From the first pages it's clear that we are in safe hands as Julia guide us through a topic that is sadly still taboo for many coaches. Full of heart, this short, introductory book demystifies and introduces a simple yet profound framework for understanding trauma. It shows how we can apply this understanding using common coaching skills. The examples show just how often survival strategies show up in our everyday work. If in your coaching you have ever encountered work addiction, perfectionism, imposter syndrome, control, bullying, 'gremlins' or felt 'stuck', buy this book; if you haven't, buy it for the day you do. I will definitely add it to the reading list on our coach training programme.*"

Helen Sieroda, Director Wise Goose School of Coaching

"*Julia has written a clear, enlightening, well grounded in theory and very practical book about how Trauma impacts identity, causing 'surviving self' behaviours in our clients, as well as in us as coaches. These behaviours are responsible for entanglement in painful and often oppressive dynamics within individuals, teams and organisations. I have introduced the model as described by Julia to clients ranging from fund managers and business owners to young entrepreneurs and older people seeking a change in direction either due to redundancy, burnout or retirement. Without fail so far, the use of this approach seems to ignite a greater connection to the 'healthy self' and with an emphasis on staying grounded in my own healthy self as the practitioner, this has made more effective coaching possible. Therapists who coach will also find much to draw on and apply in their work with clients both in counselling contexts and as coaches and consultants using an integrated approach with individuals and teams.*"

Carolyn Mumby, Executive and Personal Coach-Therapist,
Supervisor and Facilitator. Chair BACP coaching division

Contents

List of figures

Foreword

To make us aware that we have a psyche and how this psyche develops and works is of great value in a world where most people have a traumatised psyche. Only then we understand what we are doing out of our traumatised psyche and how this produces even more traumata. It is only then we might be willing to stop our trauma-surviving-strategies and to reflect on what is really good for us and what is really good for others with whom we live together on this planet.

We now also have valuable methods to explore and understand our inner world more and more. It doesn't matter in the end if we call the processes of changing our traumatised psyche psychotherapy or coaching. The most important thing is that we start doing it. I am grateful to Julia Vaughan Smith that she is sharing her knowledge and skills about how to support change processes of human beings to exit their trauma biographies and to live a life based on their healthy psyche. When we meet with our healthy parts, our traumatised parts give us back our full life potentials. I know this from my own journey, regaining piece by piece the split off parts of my psyche. It is wonderful and the best thing I ever did in my life.

Franz Ruppert, Munich, April 2019

Series preface

When we published our first title in the *Coaching in Practice* series, way back in 2007, only an exceptionally wise person could have predicted the rapid expansion of coaching. Then, it was hard to find reliable initial training and even harder to find anything more advanced. It was unclear whether it was truly possible to make a career out of coaching and the number of people working as coaches was comparatively small. Today, all that has changed, much of it for the better. There are many excellent training courses. Nationally and internationally recognised qualifications have expanded in both scope and rigour.

As a supervisor I am a personal witness to the viability of coaching as a lucrative career. There are tens of thousands of people calling themselves coaches: the word has even been adopted to cover activities as varied as parent coach, finance coach, career coach and even, as I saw in a recent article, flirting coach. Executive coaching is now an attractive second career for increasing numbers of people looking for new ways of growing their interest in the development of people.

Yet while there are many books which cater for the beginner coach, including my own book, also published by Open University Press, *Coaching Skills: The Definitive Guide to Being a Coach*, it is still the case that there are relatively few which explore and deepen more specialist aspects of the role. There is more interest in questions of ethics and boundaries, for instance in the shadowy line between therapy and coaching. There is better understanding of the mysteries of the coach–client relationship and of what makes it work – or not. There is more acceptance of the idea that every coach needs a supervisor.

This is the territory that we cover in this series. The titles range from the practicalities of developing and running a coaching business to the history of coaching, and to books which expand the range of tools, techniques, and approaches that a coach might try with teams as well as with individuals. Underlying themes are, in many titles, about the psychology of human change and why it matters so much in coaching. As I know from personal experience of running initial coach training courses, it is often hard to find enough time to cover all of these vital topics in sufficient depth.

The series is called *Coaching in Practice* because the aim is to unite theory and practice in an accessible way. The books are short, designed to be easily understood without in any way compromising on the integrity of the ideas they explore. All are written by senior coaches, in every case with many years of hands-on experience.

This series is for you if you are undertaking or completing your coaching training and perhaps in the early stages of the unpredictability, pleasures, and dilemmas that working with actual clients brings. Now that you have passed the honeymoon stage, you may have begun to notice the limitations of your approaches and knowledge. You are eager for more information and guidance. You probably know that it is hard to make the leap between being a good-enough coach and an outstanding one. Or perhaps you are a much more experienced coach thirsty for more help and challenges. You may also be one of the many people still contemplating a career in coaching. If so, these books will give you useful direction on many of the issues which preoccupy, perplex, and delight the working coach.

Jenny Rogers
Series Editor

Acknowledgements

My first thanks go to Professor Franz Ruppert, from whom I have learnt so much about myself, about psyche-trauma, and how to work therapeutically with the splits in the psyche. I am deeply grateful to him for this and for allowing me to use his model in my book. I also thank Vivian Broughton for introducing me to his work and for all I have learnt from her. Similarly, thanks to everyone I have learnt with and from in all the workshops I have been part of and those I have worked with.

I have valued and needed the support and encouragement given to me by my friends, including those who commented so helpfully on the drafts, so thank you Brian Lewis, Alexandra Smith, Laurence Jarosy, and Valerie Iles for your feedback. The book wouldn't have got going without Jenny Rogers' encouragement, and it wouldn't have got finished without her comments on the drafts and her careful editing advice. I was able to focus on the shape of the book at a writing retreat with Professor Jonathan Gosling, whose guidance helped me give it form. Early on I was given great advice by Lorna Howarth, then of the Write Factor, whose guidance and encouragement was very gratefully received.

Getting the book finished is one thing, getting it fit for the publisher is another, and Hannah Kenner's clear, detailed, and responsive guidance and support helped me know what was needed and how to do it. Thanks, too, to Trudie Byrne of Bright Blue C for her help with the graphics. Living closely with an author on days when the writing isn't going well has its challenges, as does the absence of the author when the writing is going well, so loving thanks to Don Oldham for his belief in me, his patient copy-editing of every draft, and for his advice.

Introduction

The therapy world has become increasingly more informed and aware of the causes and impact of traumatising events, especially early childhood experience and its impact on adult behaviour. I have written this book to bring that awareness to the coaching field.

My psychotherapy training and practice raised my awareness and understanding of the impact of childhood experience, and to working in a different way. I took that understanding into my coaching and supervision practice. In 2008, I trained as a family constellations facilitator, and through doing my own personal work, I understood how trauma was multi-generational and passed down through the bonding process. My trauma history starts with my grandmother whose mother died when she was eighteen months old, in childbirth. She and her siblings travelled back from Australia to Devon (in around 1886) with a relative and a wet nurse for the baby. The siblings were separated and placed with foster families. Through my family constellations work I was able to understand the impact of my grandmother on my own mother and how she, in turn, related to me as a baby, child, and adult.

In 2009, I started working with Professor Franz Ruppert and Vivian Broughton. This brought the focus of the work from the family system to my own inner dynamics. I was able to experience my survival defences and bring my trauma feelings into conscious awareness. My survival defences over my life until that time had been anxiety, denial, addiction to work, and control (over myself). Exploring my personal inner experience enabled me to recognise these defences, and what triggered them, and to face the reality of my own trauma of identity and love. While I was successful in many ways, I was struggling with these inner dynamics. Through doing my own work, and participating in the work of others, I also learnt how to be a facilitator of the process, using it with therapy clients and applying the theory to my coaching and supervision practice. This involved many hours of learning and supervision.

While in writing this book I have drawn on the work of many people in the trauma therapy field, I focus on the work of Professor Ruppert (2012, 2014, 2016; Ruppert and Banzhaf, 2018), as his theory offers a simple model for understanding the deep complexities of trauma. When I have introduced it to clients and supervisees, they quickly grasp the fundamental elements and see how it applies to coaching. I have been told it has brought a new dimension to coaching practice and that coaches applying their understanding have seen a positive impact on client outcomes.

This book is for people who work as independent coaches and supervisors, whose approach involves personal development as a means of achieving external changes in life, work, and career. It is not my intention that such coaches should become therapists; this book is to support you in becoming a more effective coach and/or supervisor.

In Chapter 1, I clarify the terminology, which is essential because the term 'trauma' is used so freely. I also talk about our developing understanding of the vulnerability of the infant in utero, as well as in the early years, to trauma, and how our environment affects our early development. Chapter 2 enlarges on that as I explore some of the neuroscience and physiology of trauma. I also cover the causal factors of developmental trauma in more detail.

Chapter 3 provides an overview of Professor Franz Ruppert's (2012) model of the split in the psyche. I clarify his use of the term 'psyche' and the split crated by trauma. This chapter looks at the trauma survival strategies and how they appear in coaching contexts. Chapters 4 and 5 expand on these ideas, specifically the constructed/adaptive survival self and the survival dynamics established as part of the trauma response. As elsewhere, there are many examples that apply this to the coaching field.

Chapter 6 focuses on leadership and teams; I also draw on the work of Earl Hopper and colleagues (2012) about team dynamics in a traumatised team. I apply this particularly to one-to-one coaching of team leaders and members from traumatised teams.

Chapter 7 explores the space that therapy and coaching share in trauma healing, and the space coaching doesn't share and should not inhabit. I talk about the wide variation in the predominance of the survival self and dynamics and what this means for coaching. I end by reflecting on what this means for supervision and personal development as a coach.

In all the chapters, I provide case examples and explore the applications to coaching. These cases are all fictional, drawn from experience but not using any direct client examples. The human condition is widely shared and any connection with any individual situation is coincidental.

This book is not a 'tool kit' for fixing trauma. It is a guide to how to understand trauma and to select and use the coaching skills and interventions already available in more appropriate and effective ways. Some readers may find it beneficial to read a chapter all the way through and then return to read it in more detail. You may like to read it with a notepad to hand or be prepared to make notes on the page. It is possible that apparently unrelated thoughts may be triggered that you want to revisit later.

1   What are we talking about?

Both the word and the idea of trauma can raise concerns and anxieties in coaches. I have had the following responses when talking about trauma within coaching circles:

> *'What's trauma got to do with coaching?'*
>
> *'Surely it's the field of therapy?'*
>
> *'Why is it relevant or useful for me?'*
>
> *'Surely, better to focus on positive thoughts?'*
>
> *'Don't use the word trauma, it will put people off.'*

In addition to these responses, I encounter confusion about the definition of trauma, as the word is used in so many ways. In this chapter, I clarify the terminology and provide an overview of trauma and its relationship with coaching. This sets the foundation for the book.

Trauma and coaching

We see the signs of trauma all around us – people living on the streets, people with addictions or mental health problem, knife crime by young gangs, and members of the armed forces returning from warzones. Although trauma is associated with each of these groups, they are rarely encountered in the coaching room.

Yet many who come into coaching, both clients and coaches, including those who appear highly successful, are traumatised. The symptoms may be less intensive than in the examples above but none the less have a negative impact on individuals and those around them. The expression of the trauma symptoms may not be so dramatic, but we meet them regularly in our work. These symptoms can get in the way of effective coaching and of personal development. It is for this reason that coaches need to learn about trauma, so they can apply that learning to their own mode of working.

If you consult any business or coaching book index, you will rarely find the word trauma listed. When I began talking about trauma to the corporate world, I was advised not to use the word as it scared people. I think that response is in part due to the association of the word itself with those most affected by their trauma and in part to a fear of the overwhelming presence of trauma. There is no option but to use the term trauma; however, a full understanding of the term and what it implies is essential. Using the term correctly helps us understand the impact on our bodies, our emotions, and our thought patterns.

Importantly, it also provides a way to think about what is happening in the 'here and now' for clients and coaches and how that might be connected to the 'there and then' of the past. To be effective, we need to understand how the shadows of the past are being cast in the present, so that we can support our clients better. When coaching clients say they want to change, these shadows may be part of what is preventing that change happening or may be driving the change wanted in unhealthy ways. This is particularly relevant where client self-awareness and inner change are part of the coaching approach.

I am not recommending that coaches reading this book become therapists or 'do therapy'. However, coaching shares a small overlap with therapy when it comes to trauma and has a contribution to make to trauma healing. Coaching isn't *therapy* because therapy usually involves a deep process of self-exploration, through which we challenge our narrative and bring painful feelings into our full awareness – safely, thus allowing healing from emotional pain. However, coaching can be *therapeutic*, if we consider it to be the achievement of healthy and favourable out-comes for the client through supporting the mobilisation of inner resources to bring about desired personal change.

Clarifying the terminology

The main challenge in talking about trauma is the terminology. The words 'trauma' and 'traumatised' are used in many ways that cause confusion and concern. For example:

- 'It was a major trauma' – the mass shootings in Las Vegas.
- 'They were highly traumatised' – the victims of the hurricanes in the Caribbean.
- 'It was a traumatic experience' – suddenly going bald as a child.
- 'It was such a trauma' – trying to find a place to park.
- 'Every day brings a new trauma' – newspaper headline from an article about keeping calm.

No wonder, then, that coaches are concerned about trauma when it is unclear what we are talking about.

To begin with, trauma does not refer to a specific event. It is not the cause but the consequence of experience. The word trauma comes from the Greek word for wound, and it is thus the 'wounds' we are left with.

Nor is it being stressed. Any individual who experiences high stress as a result of, for example, a motor accident, the sudden death of a close friend, or a burglary, will need help to return their stress levels to a normal rhythm and to accommodate the experience. However, such experiences may not result in a trauma response. Such a response occurs when the level of threat to life is highly intensive and escape is not possible, causing the stress response of fight or flight to be replaced by that of freeze and fragment.

Trauma results from experiences that are – or feel – life-threatening, and when there is no escape. The threat is such that the normal fight or flight response of the stress system 'overheats' and is thus unable to function. Instead, a freeze and numbing response takes over. This sequence of responses has a *lasting impact* on our network of internal systems: emotions, nervous system (stress hormones), neurological (brain development, memory, thought, perception) and bio-physiological processes. That is, it has a lasting impact on how we feel, experience, and respond to others, and how we think about and relate to ourselves and those around us. Our cognitive, emotional, and body systems are forever changed as part of the trauma. Trauma is a neuro-physiological-emotional networked process; it occurs within the body systems. Ruppert (2014; Ruppert and Banzhaf, 2018) refers to this as the 'psyche' and uses the term psyche-trauma to describe the complexity of response. When I use these terms in the book, this is the meaning that I adopt.

The term trauma is also correctly used in relation to physical trauma, for example, the result of an accident or attack, or major surgery. When we talk of physical trauma, we can see the wound, the blood, or the scar tissue. With psyche-trauma, we cannot see the wound directly, although we are aware of its impact. What we meet instead is the externalised result of the trauma on behaviour. This includes how we relate to others, how safe we feel, our thoughts, emotional responses, levels of stress, and our bodily experience. These are examples of 'there and then' patterns that get replayed in the 'here and now'.

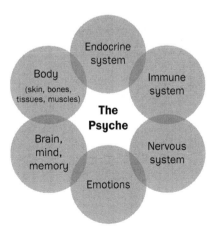

Figure 1.1 The psyche

Like a physical wound, psyche-trauma can be healed to some extent through personal commitment to deep change; without that, the wound is repeatedly re-opened or 're-infected'.

The primary cause of trauma is early childhood experience, including during the in-utero period. When I talk about trauma and coaching, this is the territory we are in and why trauma is widespread. Of course, certain life experiences (war, rape, attempted murder) can be traumatising and may also reopen earlier trauma. However, most trauma encountered in coaching will come from early experience.

The importance of early relationships

Human infants are highly vulnerable to their environment. In utero, their physiological and neurological systems are developing. An infant is vulnerable to trauma when, for example, the mother is highly stressed, as this crosses the umbilical cord into the infant, whose stress responses are also triggered. Surgery on the infant in utero can be life-saving but is likely to produce high levels of stress both in the mother and the infant. The same is true for complicated births, such as delivery by caesarean section. Once born, human infants depend on others to meet their symbiotic needs for life, including food, warmth, safety, love, and touch. As humans, our brains develop through the relationships we have with others. This starts in utero and continues into childhood, as our brains and minds are shaped through our earliest relationship with our mother, and with other close family members. This relationship is based on our needs being met, including how we are held and looked at, talked to, and engaged with. Parents who are visually impaired or unable to hear find ways of engaging with their infant to build a bonded relationship.

If these needs are not met, human infants will die. If they are met inconsistently, the lack of safety felt will produce stress levels so high they will become traumatised, and the trauma response will be triggered. Trauma results from our earliest symbiotic needs not being met, and from what we do to survive in such an environment. It is these survival adaptations that cause difficulties over time, after the immediate threat has gone, because they continue as if the threat were still there.

There are many things that can lead to trauma in utero and in early childhood. These include the psychological and physical health and well-being of the mother (primarily) and father or partner. If they are traumatised themselves or physically ill, they will find it difficult to respond consistently to the needs of the infant.

Any prolonged separation from the mother in early life will have a lasting impact and is likely to be traumatising, such as when mother or infant is ill – for example, when an infant is placed in an incubator after birth or the parents of a hospitalised child are unable to visit because of an illness. Or, it could be the result of adoption or being fostered. Unfortunately, many infants needing special care after birth are unable to have skin-to-skin contact with their mother and, instead of being held by her, will be handled by medical staff. This will be a traumatising environment for the infant.

In addition to these early experiences, some children experience physical and/or sexual abuse. Being brought up in a family where violence and rage are regular features leaves the young child terrified and feeling very unsafe. Sexual abuse of a child is the violation of a helpless victim. If the abuser is a member of the family or close community, there is also a profound betrayal of trust and lack of protection. Unfortunately, both physical and sexual abuse are more common than we would like to believe.

Because of the lasting impact of trauma, parents who were traumatised as children often find it challenging to respond to the needs of their own infants. In this way, trauma can pass from generation to generation, through the bonding process. There is also the risk of inter-generational transmission of sexual and physical abuse.

Living in poverty results in many additional stressors in people's lives. The burden placed on poorer parents who are themselves traumatised makes it hard for them to respond consistently to their child in an appropriate way. The same is true, of course, of those who uproot themselves and seek asylum or refuge elsewhere: this is a profoundly stressful and thus traumatising experience.

It is helpful here to hold in mind the concept of 'good enough mothering/parenting' (Winnicott, 1964). No parent is super-human. 'Good enough' means infants' needs are lovingly met enough of the time for them not to feel unsafe, go hungry or feel abandoned, and there is sufficient likelihood of healthy development. The wider family also has a role in providing such an environment.

The nature of the relationship between the mother and her partner also has a lasting impact on patterns of relating to others as adults. Both Bowlby (1971) and Ainsworth et al. (1979) highlighted this in relation to maternal separation and the effect on a dependent infant whose needs for love, food, warmth, touch, and safety are not met on a regular basis. These authors categorised behaviour in relationship as either secure or insecure. Insecure attachment, which is now considered to be the result of trauma, may involve avoidant, ambivalent, anxious, resistant, or chaotic behaviours in relationship. These define ways in which adults relate to others, to their work, and to themselves.

If a mother and/or her partner experienced rejection, anger, neglect, attempted abortion, or physical or sexual abuse as children, they will have established patterns of relating as children intended to keep them from further emotional and physical pain. These patterns of relating may well be carried over into their relationship with a new baby. Such parents many become anxiously dependent on the baby, smothering them with attention, or they may have minimal contact with the infant, afraid of the love they may feel – or do not feel – or they may be inconsistent in how they respond. They might 'manage' the infant with a strict regime, becoming over-protective or under-protective. They may leave the infant to cry for long periods, limiting the amount of contact they have with the child. Such traumatised parenting results in adaptive behaviours in the child, and these trauma survival defences can last throughout life unless we set about understanding and changing them. The trauma is therefore passed on.

Trauma can be passed down through the generations unless individuals work intensively on their unconscious defensive behaviour. Trauma survival defences in adults include being either extremely dependent on others, clingy, and anxious to please, or being fiercely independent – rejecting help or closeness, not being able to maintain a lasting and close relationship with another person. Some such adults may be experienced by others as chaotic and confusing in how they relate, being 'all over the place' – even exposing themselves, unknowingly, to danger. Trauma in the parent, therefore, produces trauma in the child, which results in insecure attachment patterns that continue into adulthood.

Being a victim of a traumatising environment

Trauma results from environmental impacts, which for babies and young children includes the people they are most dependent on. Individuals can become traumatised by the intentional or unintentional acts of others, leaving them emotionally and/or physically vulnerable.

Although the perpetrators of emotional/physical abuse are sometimes strangers, as in episodes of violent rage or warfare, it is more likely to be someone known to and trusted by the victim. Whatever the circumstances, the recipient of the abuse is unable to escape. If the traumatising environment is that of the close family, and being dependent on the adults, the child will have nowhere else to go. Trauma involves victims, who are the recipients, and perpetrators in relationship with one another. It is therefore sometimes referred to as relational trauma – trauma as a result of relationship.

Life events at any age, whether war, fire, famine, or life-threatening experiences, involving strangers or those known to us, are traumatising for many. However, individuals respond to such events in widely differing ways. If, for example, two people experience a terrorist attack, or a life-changing motor accident, one might be emotionally traumatised (using the correct definition) while the other might be highly stressed and scared, requiring emotional and physical rehabilitation but not leaving them with lasting damage. How an individual responds will be influenced by how imminent they felt death was, as well as their early childhood experience. If, for example, they are already traumatised, such an event will have the effect of re-traumatising them. Recovery is also influenced by the nature of support available and that engaged with, which in turn can be influenced by trauma survival defences.

Survival responses to the environment

In order to survive our traumatising early environment, we develop responses to the trauma so as to suppress the pain and to prevent further hurt. If you think of the trauma as a wound, the centre of the pain resulting from the experience, these survival mechanisms represent a means of distracting ourselves from the pain (by trying to ensure the same thing doesn't happen again) or of covering over the wound so that it doesn't hurt so much, but at the same time preventing it from healing.

Relationships in the 'here and now' can be experienced, unconsciously, as being as unsafe as earlier relationships in the 'there and then'. Even when they are not, we use the same 'there and then' defences to manage the 'here and now' experience, often in ways that are not helpful to us as adults.

There is a tendency for individuals to repeat patterns from the past and to find themselves – again and again – in relationships that are harmful. This applies to relationships in the working environment as it does other relationships. We may, for example, find ourselves working for or with people who knowingly or unknowingly do us emotional or possibly physical harm – the latter through overwork. Some organisations are routinely uncaring and mistreat their employees. Even if we are not repeating patterns from the past, we can find ourselves unexpectedly working in a relational environment that has some elements of the 'there and then', which triggers the trauma survival defences.

Trauma leaves individuals with toxic levels of stress hormones, which might come to feel 'normal' and which continue to have an impact on their body systems. We use a range of strategies to manage such high levels of stress, but sometimes only make matters worse. This also leaves us vulnerable to further stressors in the environment.

The feelings of fear, terror, rage, and deep sense of loneliness that are associated with trauma are kept deeply hidden and are controlled by the survival defence strategies. However, at times we will meet these feelings when a client suddenly experiences deep distress that appears to 'come from nowhere', often leaving them feeling ashamed or embarrassed. It can also be shocking for the coach, as is described here by a coach in supervision:

> '*I was quite shocked, we were talking and I made an intervention, I'm not sure what it was, and she started breathing shallowly and very fast, as if she might have a panic attack; she seemed to have disappeared, wasn't in the room with me. I didn't really know what to do. I found myself concerned as we didn't have long left in the session.*'

Client histories

We hear about the history of trauma when clients disclose their childhood stories. When we understand the likely causes of trauma in childhood, we listen differently to clients' autobiographies. We can listen out for life events that might have caused a lasting impact and for possible survival defences. We can never be sure, and we shouldn't diagnose, however we can use the curiosity of coaching to hold a question open about whether something 'there and then' has a connection with the 'here and now' of clients' coaching intentions. Such examples might include loss of contact with the mother (through illness, hers or theirs, or fostering); loss of close attachment figures through death or divorce; sexual, emotional or physical abuse; bullying at school and/or being at boarding school. For example:

> *'My father was a violent man.'*
>
> *'My mother was very ill when I was a child and I was cared for by a series of aunts when I was one and two years old.'*
>
> *'My family were very poor indeed and my mother really struggled.'*
>
> *'My sister died when she was seven and I was four.'*
>
> *'I had TB and was in hospital for two years. My parents couldn't visit much.'*
>
> *'My mother died when I was two.'*
>
> *'I was sent to boarding school when I was seven.'*
>
> *'My sister was born with a disability and needed a lot of hospital treatment. She is two years younger than me.'*
>
> *'I don't remember much.'*

In coaching, the autobiography narrative often appears to start in mid-childhood. In therapy, there is a greater focus on what happened early on, around conception, birth, and the first few years. Thus in coaching we may not hear all the indications of possible trauma. However, the survival defence systems will indicate its presence.

The idea that we had a 'very happy childhood' often does not withstand scrutiny; all childhoods have their challenges, although not all of them are traumatising. All children in a family have a different experience of their childhood; no two children are brought up the same. Birth order, gender, and the child's character all make a difference, as do the circumstances around the pregnancy, birth, and early years.

Sometimes our clients become emotional telling us their history. Our role is to give space to that telling, to listen, to acknowledge, and to witness what we are told. We should not attempt to rescue or close the emotion down. We need to be able to bear it. Others may tell us their story with no or little emotion. Either way, they are giving us useful information about the 'there and then', which may be valuable in exploring the 'here and now' of what they are bringing to coaching.

Coaches may, unconsciously, communicate they don't want too much distress brought into the room, from a fear that they can't cope with it. While coaching does not aim to encourage distress, if it is present in clients we need to make the process feel safe enough for them to share that distress. By not doing so, the coaching will be superficial in nature.

Survival defences in coaching

It is primarily the survival defence mechanisms that we meet in coaching in our experience of the client and in our response to them. The impact is felt in coaching when the work is not going well and/or feels challenging to us. We also meet it in clients who feel stuck or unable to make any changes, and who are driven to continue with how they are managing their work and life, as the following examples, described by coaches, illustrate:

> '*My work with G feels very stuck, we are getting nowhere, I think I should suggest we just stop. I don't think I have the skills or experience needed to make this work better.*'

> '*The time seems to go so slowly; I keep looking at the clock and waiting for the session to be over.*'

> '*M always wants to change the times of our sessions, and often when I arrive, she tells me she only has an hour before she has to leave, which I find very frustrating.*'

> '*R has been accused of bullying at work. He denies it, says he was just getting the work done and that the accuser needs to "man up". I don't like him very much, which is wrong I know, but I don't.*'

> '*P seems very caught up with running around after her boss, taking on more work and working much longer hours, but defends that as being necessary.*'

> '*D says he works all the time and every evening, never having time for himself or his family. When we explore how he might shift that, he can't see how, and if we find some small steps, when he returns he has taken on more work, not reduced it.*'

> '*I just don't feel I have any connection with her. It is as if she is not really in the room with me. She is distant and distracted and nothing I do seems to get through that. I feel like shouting at her just to get a response, but I don't suppose that will work either.*'

The survival dynamics of clients include relationship problems at work, not for the first time, feelings of being unable to leave a profession or organisation and/or a propensity for rescuing those around them while becoming exhausted and resentful. Such dynamics may result in feeling a victim and being unable to act, being accused of bullying others, or being experienced as aggressive or unempathetic by those around them.

The defence mechanisms of clients can leave coaches feeling criticised or attacked, their interventions ignored or rejected. We might experience clients as distant and avoidant, as cold or dependent. They may feel the coaching is confusing, frustrating, boring or superficial. We may be tempted to retaliate, having had our own trauma touched upon and our survival defences activated. In the following instance, this included aggression on the part of the coach:

> '*The client was so aggressive towards me, rejected everything I offer, I found myself being very sharp in the session. Afterwards I felt very aggressive towards her.*'

Or we might respond by doing all the work or rescuing clients from their inaction:

> '*I feel sorry for H and want to do what I can to help, it is so difficult for him. I have changed the times to suit him, they are not great for me, but I feel it is important and I have been doing a lot of research on his behalf as he just doesn't have the time.*'

> '*I find myself doing all the work. I am continually thinking of what exercises might be useful to use, as we seem to make no progress.*'

We might get caught up in a 'game' of survival played out between the defence systems of the client or organisation and those of our own, because we are using 'there and then' systems to manage the 'here and now'. The example below illustrates how that may be experienced:

> '*I don't feel happy about this contract, there is something about it that I didn't like at the time, I feel I am being set up in some way, but it is an important contract for me and I want to be seen to be someone they want to use again.*'

Examples of our own survival defences therefore include working 'too hard', using too many exercises or tools, and talking too much – or talking very little and waiting for the session to end. We might feel deskilled and question our competence, so rush to refer. We might find ourselves being passive-aggressive to the client or rescuing; we might pull away from the client or do more for them out of session time than we know we should; we might become caught up in organisational dynamics and feel we can't get out of them. We might feel helpless and hurt by clients.

Understanding trauma can help us identify and explore these responses to clients and return ourselves to a more effective coaching position. The coach in the example below is talking to her supervisor about a client whose behaviour suggests an insecure attachment pattern:

> '*I had to talk to you, this client is so difficult, I am finding him very challenging. He dismisses or ridicules everything I suggest, challenges the tools I propose using, won't sit still, keeps moving around the room.*'

In exploring this issue, the coach recognised that she felt very challenged by the client's behaviour. She had been very abrupt and sharp with the client at times because she had felt rejected and insulted. She said she didn't want to keep meeting with the client.

Here, the client appears to push away help and the possibility of contact with another person by being aggressive and rude. The risk is that the coach, because of her trauma, may either fall into a victim attitude, thinking '*I'm a poor coach, anyone else would be able to handle this client, it's how I am approaching the client, I chose the wrong interventions*'; or get caught up in the fight and become passive-aggressive or openly aggressive in response. Either way, coaching has stopped. In the supervision discussion, the coach went back to the contracting and what the client was attending for. This client was successful in his field but had been referred to coaching because of relationship problems with his team. His behaviour with the coach gave a good insight into what he might be like with colleagues at work. Once he realised what was happening to her, she was able to think about what coaching interventions might be useful. She noted that the client did come for each session and so assumed that part of him wanted to be there and explored what she needed for herself in order not to 'lose her shape'.

Sometimes we can be confused by clients who say they want to change but appear to resist making it happen, as the following coach describes:

> '*The client's goal is that she wants to find a better work–life balance. She says she is working up to eighty hours a week, every evening and weekend; she's not sleeping well and is exhausted. I've tried everything, we do goal setting, reality testing, explore what feels possible and doable, levels of motivation. We agree some shifts and she leaves saying she is going to put them into action, then when she comes back not only has she not been able take those actions but she has taken on even more work.*'

This is an addiction to work, a survival defence behaviour, with no motivation to change. The coach had become caught up in doing whatever she could to find a way to change the addiction behaviour without recognising it as such. We can hypothesise that the client was using addiction to work to suppress her emotional distress from the 'there and then', which is why she was resisting letting go of that behaviour.

Had the coach explored the client's level of confidence, she might have heard the client rate it at around 2–3 out of 10. A different conversation may then follow but with the same possible overall outcome. The idea that there was 'one thing I didn't try that might have worked' can be part of continuing to try to change the client when they appear unable to enact that change themselves. Reflection and action learning are an important part of professional practice and supervision and will help us disentangle what is going on within us.

Sometimes in supervision, a coach will say that a client has said something that 'came from nowhere', leaving them unsure of what they should have done:

> '*I have found it hard to work with S, the coaching feels very stuck, and 'S' says she feels stuck without choices. In the middle of the last session she told me that she had been sexually abused by a close family friend over a three-year period as a child and said: "I have dealt with all of that" and it didn't need to be part of our work. I felt very shocked but said something empathetic, I thought, which S pushed away. I felt very conflicted, as it seemed like a big thing to share but also felt I should respect her saying she didn't want it to be part of the work. So we moved on.*'

On reflection the coach said the lack of emotion had disturbed her, as had her own shock at the revelation coming from nowhere. What should we do? We could invite the client to explore what, if any, connection there might be between her experience and the 'here and now'; or ask what helped her deal with that experience. It is possible that as the client has raised it, that there is some connection. If we can apply some skilled responses, she might feel safe enough to consider the connection, keeping focused on what it is she wants for her well-being and life now. Or she might not, and it is not for us to push a client to explore something against their will. In supervision, the coach can explore her own responses and how to prevent herself using survival responses connected to her own 'there and then'.

Mental health

We also meet the trauma of clients when they tell us they have an emotional or mental health problem which they may have had for some time. The understanding in the trauma field is that most forms of diagnosed or undiagnosed mental ill health, such as depression, bipolar disorder, personality disorder, anxiety states, and addictions, have their roots in early childhood trauma and are forms of trauma survival.

Many clients and coaches feel shame at having, or having had, a mental health problem and keep it hidden, including myself. I suffered an extensive period of depression, anxiety, and anorexia in my twenties. I now understand those to be trauma survival responses, but I still feel deep shame at admitting I had mental health issues. It is a sad reflection of society that this is the case. However, many fear that their career prospects may be threatened if 'people were to know'. Fortunately, I was working in health care at the time and received a lot of support. Some coaches feel uncomfortable talking about mental and emotional health and so avoid doing so. However, if our clients are experiencing emotional and mental health problems, such as depression, anxiety, high stress, or have a diagnosis and have had or are having treatment, it is helpful to know that. We can also explore with clients if, and in what ways, their symptoms may impact on the coaching.

Jenny Rogers (2017) has written of how she came to realise after many years of practice that she had never talked to clients about their mental and emotional health as part of their initial session together. She suggests that when using the Wheel of Life model (Whitworth et al., 1998), we add mental/emotional health to the health segment as a stimulus to having these conversations. Rogers talks about what useful information it brought into the work which otherwise might not have been disclosed.

Trauma is part of the human condition

In his book *In the Realm of the Hungry Ghosts: Close encounters with addiction* (2013), Gabor Maté speaks of the myth of 'normal' and the idea that there are two groups of people: those who are traumatised and who require a diagnosis and treatment, and those who are unaffected. He states clearly that is not the case – instead, we are all on a continuum, both us and our clients. The message is, this is not about 'other people' or the most vulnerable or disturbed. Childhood trauma is widely shared across class, race, and socio-economic status. We meet the impact of it in our coaching rooms often and in many ways.

Working with trauma in clients and ourselves is the 'norm' for coaching, not the exception. The extent to which the trauma feelings are present, or the survival self is dominant in someone's life in the 'here and now', varies greatly. With some clients, it will barely show itself, if present at all. With others, it will be present but with understanding can be worked through in the coaching process. And with others, the survival defences will predominate, making coaching challenging or even unhelpful. Of those who access coaching, a small number will be so affected that coaching can't work. The same goes for coaches: some will find they are caught up in their defences most of the time; others with specific clients only.

Healthy resources

It is recognised by trauma therapists that traumatised individuals retain the capacity to respond to 'here and now' experience without using the patterns laid down in the 'there and then' trauma pain and defence dynamics. The extent of this capacity depends on the strength of the trauma response, on the cognitive-emotional ability to reflect on experience and on the use of stress management techniques, such as deep breathing, mindfulness, and meditation.

All adults have resources available to them, both internally and externally, that weren't available to them as children and which they can draw on to bring about a different response in the 'here and now'. We can, for example, reflect on the connection between what we are experiencing now and what happened in the past. The resources we habitually turn to in the case of trauma are the survival defences, which are well established neuropathways. However, we can explore the resources not caught up in the trauma response and lay down new pathways. Being able to do so is likely to bring about healthier outcomes for us in terms of our well-being and relationships, including our relationship with work.

The focus of coaching is on accessing these resources. We cannot coach the survival defence systems – they are not interested in change. Personal development can only happen with the non-trauma-related resources. However, this means that we need to be willing and able to bear some of the pain from the 'there and then'. Understanding some of the links between the past and the present helps with this, together with the knowledge that as adults we are not dependent children, we have other choices available to us.

Grief

I said at the beginning of this chapter that some experiences cause high stress but are not traumatising in the way I have been describing. Grieving the loss of someone close, as an adult, is a normal response to loss. The grief may be emotionally painful and difficult as it progresses; it may bring increased levels of stress, too. Neither grief nor high levels of stress are necessarily traumatising, even though emotional support may be needed to work through them.

However, loss might be re-traumatising for someone who suffered a significant attachment loss in childhood, such as the loss of a parent at an early age and the child was not given emotional support to deal with it. In such circumstances, the remaining parent and other family members will also be grieving and may fail to give the grieving and confused child the level of emotional support they need. As an adult, therefore, that child might re-experience the pain from the 'there and then' along with the grief from the 'here and now' loss – and the grief will be more intense and may be hard to process. This is not an area for coaching unless the coach has specific grief counselling training.

When we are working with a client who is deeply grieving and in mourning, we have coaching responses available to us which would not be considered grief counselling. For example, we might ask:

> 'How are you doing?'
>
> 'What additional help might be useful to you?'
>
> 'What might we need to be mindful of as we continue with our work here?'

If clients decide to continue with the coaching, then the grief will have an impact and we need to explore that with the client. The client may make a link between the 'here and now' and the 'there and then' that may have some meaning for them. Or, they may want to take a break from coaching to process the emotional work that may be needed in counselling.

Keeping coaching

At times, you may be concerned about a client and feel unprepared to deal with the issues the client raises. You may feel that your training has not prepared you for this particular territory. It is right to be mindful about working within your levels of competence and speak with a coaching supervisor.

For some coaches, their anxiety and trauma survival defences get in the way and they stop coaching. Instead, they may become inactive or overactive, or avoidant or directive. They may slip into faux-counselling. Less experienced coaches are more susceptible to this, as their ability to use coaching skills and techniques is not yet fully developed. However, even seasoned coaches may also stop coaching when their trauma is activated.

This is where supervision becomes such a valuable resource for coaches. Working with a supervisor or peers in a supervision group provides an opportunity to reflect on our responses and explore what was going on for us. In the UK, most accrediting bodies expect coaches to receive supervision from someone who is appropriately trained or accredited, as part of professional development, and for the protection of both client and coach. This is good practice. The trauma survival dynamics can be strong in ourselves and our clients and we can become 'blind' to them. Working with others in a supervisory relationship helps us to see these more clearly and therefore return to a proper and more effective coaching process.

Many years ago, when setting up a coaching service with colleagues, and afterwards when designing and teaching coach training programmes, clear principles were used to shape coaching. These principles can get distorted by coaches' trauma survival responses.

Principle	How it might get distorted
Contracting clearly with clients frames our work with them. We are clear about what we can offer and the boundaries to the work.	When trauma survival is activated, the contracting process can be poorly worked through or ignored. Something distracted us from doing this fully. As a supervisor, one of my frequent questions is, 'what is the client coming for?'

Respecting clients' resourcefulness – that they have the resources they need to bring about the change they seek. Our role is to help them access and use those resources.	Coaches can step into rescuing clients, or tell them what to do, or give them advice or give up on them. These are defence responses.
Coaching is client-led – the clients set the agenda and are the ones whose motivation and confidence are essential to their change process.	Coaches can take over the agenda or become passive bystanders from fear of taking over the agenda. They fail to raise observations or reflections that challenge clients' agenda in service of the clients' espoused desired outcomes.
Coaching is future-focused – it is about acting in the present in ways that will bring about desired outcomes in the future.	The present is all we have to work with when it comes to change. Escaping to an illusory future, denying the reality of the present, or becoming distracted by the much-repeated narratives of the past are survival mechanisms for avoiding dealing with the reality of the present.
Coaching is goal-orientated; it harnesses motivation and sets the direction for the work.	Through the trauma survival processes, goal-setting can be distorted when it is not connected with clients' healthy/non-traumatised resources.
Coaching is about change.	One of the dilemmas for both coaching and therapy is that clients are often ambivalent about change, wanting it and wanting things to stay the same. This is a survival response.

There are many valuable skills, techniques, and tools that can be used in coaching. Experience enables us to use these skilfully and to pick the best interventions for the moment. Being aware of trauma in ourselves and our clients does not require us to develop new skills or tools unless we are not competent in those that are essential for effective coaching. The core skills, techniques, and attitudes for working with trauma are:

Attentive listening without the chatter in our heads, instead listening to words, observing emotions, body language, and what is not being said.	Asking powerful questions: used effectively, these are aimed at the non-traumatised resources.
Coaches' capacity for being fully present and grounded in contact with themselves and their body.	Reflecting, sharing feedback and observations in a way that is useful to the client.
Asking permission.	Self-awareness, authenticity, curiosity.
Clarifying, acknowledging, validating.	Acceptance, non-judgemental.

We do, however, need to understand what helps clients' self-awareness of their trauma survival defences and what helps self-healing. Understanding what trauma is and how it presents helps us do that.

With trauma it is important to respect professional and personal boundaries – that is, not to lapse into a social or intimate relationship, not to touch a client without permission, instead remaining consistent, trustworthy, and offering a place in which clients feel safe. Many individuals with childhood trauma have had their boundaries violated and many can quickly feel unsafe. Such individuals may not be strong in protecting their boundaries, and so may invite boundaries to be crossed. Coaches need to be aware of boundary issues and maintain them professionally. Always talk to your supervisor or peer supervision group if you notice a shift in the boundaries to the work.

2 The internalisation of trauma

We are vulnerable to trauma from the very beginning of our lives. Our stress hormone responses are activated, and memories laid down. The early relationships we have not only shape how our brain develops but also our ideas about ourselves. In this chapter, I look at the neuroscience and physiology associated with trauma, so that you may understand the impact on brain development, stress, memory, and ideas about ourselves and how this may show in coaching. I also introduce the concept of trauma biography, or the cumulative impact of traumatising experience.

While we cannot change what happened to us in early life, as adults we can become aware of the impact on us in the 'here and now' and what choices we have available to us now. To be able to make links between the 'there and then' and the 'here and now' with clients, we need to have an appreciation of the impact of experience so that we can hear the autobiography more fully and appreciate some of the trauma presentation in coaching.

Brain development

Our vulnerability starts from conception. This is clear from the neuroscience of attachment trauma and the impact on brain development, toxic stress, and memory. It had earlier been assumed that infants in utero did not suffer psyche-trauma even though it was recognised that the earliest relationships had a significant impact on brain development.

The brain develops from the first two weeks of life in utero and continues with a major growth spurt in the third part of pregnancy and in the first three years of life. Human babies are born with their brains only partly developed because, if fully developed, the skull would be too large for a vaginal delivery. The brain stem and limbic system develop first. These are often referred to as the 'reptilian brain' and the 'emotional brain', respectively. Both are involved in sensing and responding to danger and the activation of the immature but developing endocrine and stress response systems. Elements of the emotional brain are concerned with processing emotion and storing memory of experience.

The cortex, the outer layer of the brain, develops in utero. It is estimated that 250,000 brain cells are created every minute, with pathways between them, and that 100 billion brain cells are present at birth. The frontal cortex, that part of the brain that distinguishes us as higher primates, develops after birth in relationship with the main caregiver. This is the part of the brain concerned with identity, moral judgement, rational thought, and decision-making. It is also associated with how we manage emotion and learn self-control.

The brain has a right and a left hemisphere. The right hemisphere develops first in utero, allowing for emotional regulation, memory, and neurological connection with the body. As infants we are right-hemisphere-dependent until around two years of age, when the left hemisphere develops alongside language. Trauma affects the development of the right hemisphere and how it connects with the left hemisphere. This can result in the neural connections between the body, mind, and emotions being fragmented, leaving adults unable to connect with their body and the emotional information it can provide.

The environment for this developing brain is initially the womb, part of the maternal system. What the mother experiences will also be experienced by her baby. If she is stressed, owing to her pregnancy or general health, the baby will also be stressed. The stress hormones pass through the umbilical cord and the impact of high levels of stress hormones in the baby brings the trauma response. After birth, the environment is that of relationship with others. The frontal cortex expands during playful interaction with the mother and through social interaction. Its growth is diminished or damaged if these are missing, and results in relationship difficulties, a lack of self-regulation, and issues around identity and personality throughout life.

Through these interactions, we gain a sense of being a person in our own right, not an object or a projection of the needs of others. This is achieved through 'limbic resonance' – that is, when mothers or primary caregivers communicate loving emotional messages non-verbally to the infant through touch, facial expression, and eye contact. This is received by the right hemisphere of the infant, and is referred to as 'attunement' between mother and baby. Attunement is essential for attachment bonding and the infant's development. Mothers who are traumatised themselves are less able to achieve this connection and their inability to attune activates a trauma response in the infant. When we, as coaches, experience good contact with the client, feeling our presence with them, and connecting with them, we are attuned with them. As with primary caregivers, our own trauma may make this less achievable.

In addition to the development of the brain and neural pathways, the heart and intestines, both of which develop in utero and are fully formed at birth, carry an extensive network of nerve cells connected with the brain. The vagus nerve runs from the brain stem to the stomach and gut – this is the basis for our 'gut instinct'. Where the environment is traumatising, this nervous system will be highly activated, and continues to be so, which is why these organs are affected by chronic levels of stress hormones.

It is for these reasons that infants are so vulnerable to the emotional environment in which they grow and develop from conception onwards. Humans learn early on about safety, trust, how lovable we are, and how to survive as a highly dependent infant and young child. The relevance of this to coaching is that it helps us to appreciate that very early experience can produce lasting trauma. The impact is felt in the relationships adults go on to have. It is also felt in the relationship individuals have with their inner world, which may result in difficulties knowing what they want, or in being confident about what they feel and experience.

It is important also to recognise that early trauma occurs before we develop language, so that our memories are unconscious and not available to recall by thought or pictures. Consequently, early traumatising experiences may not appear in our autobiography. If they do, they will be narratives attributed to individuals by others and not their direct experiences.

Stress and trauma

Although I stated in Chapter 1 that being stressed isn't trauma, trauma and stress are closely intertwined. Psyche-trauma arises when the normal stress response to danger of fight or flight, which results in an increase in heart rate and blood flow to the muscles, 'overheats' and the system 'shuts down', prompting numbness, immobility or freezing (Figure 2.1). It also results in dissociation, whereby the connections with emotions and body sensations break down. The neuropathways shut down from engaging with the reality of the 'here and now'. Our connection with our body experience is reduced. There is a submission to the danger, preparing for the threat to happen. This is what a mouse does when threatened by a cat – it 'plays' dead. Such submission also brings shame. This process causes memories of the experience to be stored in a fragmented way, thus recall memory of traumatising experience is not available. People may sense that something happened but not possess a 'picture or sound recording' to call on.

Babies in utero and in early life are vulnerable to this response, as they can neither fight or flee. They have nowhere they can go, they cannot escape the danger. They are flooded with the alarm signals and stress hormone responses.

Being traumatised leaves us in a state of toxic stress, whereby we continue to experience high levels of stress and anxiety that we soon take to be 'normal'. The body continues to act as if the danger is always present, meaning individuals are

Freeze
Numbness
Dissociation
Submission
Fragmented memory
Shame

Figure 2.1 The trauma response

hypervigilant and alert. The 'there and then' danger is projected into the 'here and now'. Toxic stress has long-term implications for health and well-being, as it affects the immune, endocrine, cardiac, digestive, and skeletal systems of the body. It is also exhausting to live with such stress, since it compromises our capacity for rest.

In a healthy brain, there is a good flow of information and energy between the frontal lobe and the limbic system and reptilian brain, which is necessary for self-regulation and stress management. Trauma compromises this process and has a lasting impact on the levels of stress hormones present. When the connections are effective, the frontal lobe can be used for rational thought to assess the true level of danger in the 'here and now' in response to an unconscious 'danger alert' from the limbic system. In this way, we can moderate the triggers from the alarm system and our stress levels return to normal.

This process for connecting these parts of the central nervous system may be poorly developed in childhood, either because of trauma or a failure to help the infant learn self-regulation, which is traumatising in itself. Infants are unable to use their own processes for self-regulation, as the frontal lobe is still developing. They need their mother/primary caregiver to provide the regulation for them through calming, soothing, and reassuring communication, including touch. If the mother or primary caregiver has problems managing their own anxiety and if their stress levels are highly activated around the infant, they will be unable to provide this regulation.

We meet some signs of this toxic stress and diminished self-regulation in the coaching room, as the following three coaches describe:

> 'Angie is someone who appears to be agitated a lot of the time. She says she feels stressed but also says she feels depressed and exhausted. Sitting with her, I could see her fidget a lot. She talks very quickly and then goes silent, as if she has disappeared and isn't really in the room with me. It is a strange experience being with her.'

> 'John says he thrives on stress, that he builds things into his life to keep his stress levels flying. He says he likes the adrenaline rush. But he also says he can't sleep and feels very driven. He talks a lot about "good stress".'

> 'What I notice about Mary is that she doesn't seem to have a way of resting. She talks of being active the whole time, I think it stops her feeling emotionally vulnerable.'

The lasting high stress associated with trauma brings hypervigilance, hyper-activity, distress, shallow breathing, and sleeplessness. It can also involve depression, chronic fatigue or exhaustion, poor digestion, and a poor connection with the body. Often, individuals swing between hyperarousal and feelings of depression.

These are the impacts of the sympathetic and parasympathetic systems within the autonomic nervous system.

In Angie's case, she is also dissociating in the room. Dissociation is part of a hyperstressed response from the 'there and then' in the 'here and now'. This can occur in a session, albeit rarely, if the trauma feelings are stimulated. It is a way of shutting them out. At the same time, there is a disconnection with others. If clients dissociate in a session, you will feel as if they are 'not there' and they will appear distant. When you notice this is happening, it is helpful to speak to the client, using their name frequently, and encourage them to talk and come back into connection with you. For example:

> 'Angie, I notice you feel agitated a lot of the time and that now you have gone quiet. What is happening with you right now?'

If dissociation is used frequently in adulthood to block out distressing feelings, the consequent lack of awareness of the body and its needs can lead someone to over-work until exhaustion, overriding the physical symptoms of stress, and so 'press on regardless'.

John, one of the clients referred to above, thrives on stress and has developed a way to explain this. However, it is time-limited in its effectiveness. We all rely on energy and motivation to tackle challenging work but once the stress responses are activated, sleep is likely to be affected as is appetite. Our ability to function is based on our relationship with others and their willingness to put up with our behaviour. People who are highly stressed can only function if they have a team around them willing to put up with their agitation, demands, and possible unreliability. Similarly, if due to chronic stress a person is cut off from any emotional connection with what is going on for them in the workplace, colleagues will have to do the emotional work for them.

Any lifestyle that involves creating additional stress will have unhealthy physiological consequences, especially for our endocrine, immune, cardiac, and digestive systems. There is no 'good stress', other than the stress response to actual danger. What John is doing is living on the rush of adrenaline as an addiction. We can't have that rush of adrenaline without the counterbalance of the parasympathetic system, which brings exhaustion, numbness, and depression.

If Angie, John, and Mary are open to exploring their high levels of stress, we can ask them a range of questions:

> 'What have you found helps you reduce the levels of stress and anxiety you experience? How can you do more of that?'

> 'How familiar is the level of stress you are feeling?'

> 'When was the last time you felt calm and peaceful? Where were you and what was happening around you?'

We should also be aware of how clients are breathing. Are they just breathing with the top of their lungs? We can get an idea of clients' breathing from how they are talking and how their shoulders might be moving with their breathing. If I notice shallow breathing, a sign of a stress reaction, I will share my observation and check whether that is also the experience of the client. This can lead to a discussion about breathing and the imparting of some information about stress and anxiety levels and self-regulation. Resources are available on the internet and YouTube about abdominal breathing as a means of self-regulation.

If clients want to develop their capacity for self-regulation and calming, they will need to invest time in learning and using mindfulness, meditation practice, Tai Chi or abdominal breathing. There is evidence that mindfulness, taught by an accredited teacher, has a positive impact on stress regulation and is as effective as antidepressants (Davis, 2018). There are also therapeutic processes that focus on stress discharge – that is, releasing some of the toxic stress through body-based therapy. Some also help clients build up images of a safe place internally where they can 'take themselves' when they feel their stress levels rising (Levine, 1997).

Post-traumatic stress

As we have seen, toxic stress is part of the lasting impact of trauma. Post-traumatic stress can be a lasting effect of early childhood experience or in response to a life-threatening experience in adulthood. Post-traumatic stress disorder (PTSD) is a diagnostic category used by practitioners to make a diagnosis and to prescribe treatment interventions. Many people in the field of trauma consider that experiences in adult life, however terrifying they may be, have the impact they do because they activate the unconscious memory of earlier trauma. This can be the case for military personnel diagnosed with PTSD, and for any intensive life-threatening experience, such as a motor accident. This is why two people in similar near fatal motor accidents can respond so differently to their experience.

Traumatic stress often presents with dissociation from the present with terrifying memory flashbacks. These flashbacks can be auditory, visual, somatic or emotional in nature, and there is always hyperarousal. We lose the ability to differentiate memory from present reality, so memories are experienced as if they are happening in the 'here and now'. During the intense experience being remembered, the area in the brain connected with language can go 'off-line'. If this occurs, the individual in question will not be able to voice what they are experiencing. Here are two coaches talking about clients who spoke of flashbacks from life-threatening or traumatising experiences:

> *'Kate talked of having flashbacks of seeing her daughter dying in the car seat beside her [they had been in a terrible car accident] and had been unable to reach her because she was unable to move and couldn't touch her daughter or speak.'*

> *'David said he still has flashbacks of being sexually abused at school by*
> *one of the teachers. He said he starts to tremor, feels cold and clammy as*
> *if he is going to vomit. He can see his teacher ready for him as if it is*
> *happening now.'*

Everyone who experiences post-traumatic stress or who have a diagnosis of PTSD need specialised help to recover. This is not the territory of coaching unless the coach is appropriately trained and qualified. However, all coaches can support our clients in finding and accessing the help they need to process the experience.

Rarely, clients might become re-traumatised in a session. This is an acute re-stimulation of stress hormone responses. Clients become cold, possibly shaky, dissociate, and start to breathe rapidly. If this should happen, keep calm and ensure you are managing your own breathing. Use the client's name often and remind them where they are. Maintain verbal contact with them. Avoid using touch, as clients' responses are unpredictable. When clients return from this dissociated place, they may feel shame and will be shaky. Offer them a glass of water and give them time to recover – keep focused on helping them return their breathing to normal. Check what they plan to do when they leave the session and advise them to sit somewhere quietly for a while. Ask them if they would like to call someone to come and take them home.

Memory and trauma

Early memories associated with traumatising experiences are not available to cognitive recall because they are out of conscious awareness. Such 'implicit' memories carry the emotional and sensory information of the experience and are connected to the physical experience of the body. Memory that is available to cognitive recall is laid down from around two years of age, when language is developing, and the coding and storage systems are being established. This is 'explicit memory', which provides the pictures, sounds, and experiences that we can recall as a narrative.

Some memory is triggered when external conditions mirror those of the time when the memory was laid down and can arise from either implicit or explicit memory. This is termed 'state-dependent memory'. As a simple example, before revisiting a city, I couldn't remember its layout at all. However, once there I could remember my way around easily. At a deeper level, trauma memory can be released in the same way. If it is implicit memory, there will be emotional or body-based experience linked to the early trauma. If explicit in nature, it may also lead to recall of images or sounds. This might be experienced by a woman during childbirth or vaginal examination, for example, if she was sexually abused as a child. It can also happen when we return to the location of a traumatising experience such as sexual or physical abuse.

Trauma memory is by nature fragmented as part of the trauma dissociation response. Explicit and implicit memories are stored in a disorganised and unconnected way. Therefore, we do not have a coherent narrative to relate what happened to us and memory recall may seem vague and uncertain. The processing for the storage of explicit memory can be disabled during traumatising experiences. As a result, adults may have no explicit memory recall of having been abused as a child, even when there is documented evidence that abuse did occur (Freyd, 1996). The implicit memory will be there but can be hard to access without skilled help. Family narratives often serve to keep trauma memory well hidden. Individuals also suppress explicit memories because of the associated shame and emotional pain.

In coaching, there is a greater reliance on explicit memory and clients often describe memories to us. At times, they are not sharing memory but a narrative they have been given by others, for example:

> '*I'm told I nearly drowned as a young child, I don't know what happened, but my parents were very shaken by it.*'

> '*My mother died when I was eighteen months old, but my aunt looked after me and they said I was happy with her; so, I don't think it had a big impact on me.*'

Such narratives might have been shaped by the teller in ways intended to 'protect the child' or 'protect the teller'. The individual's memory from childhood is, of course, stored in implicit memory, which can be triggered in the 'here and now'.

Explicit memory, unlike implicit memory, is open to distortion due to the conflation of events, imagination, perception, what we've been told, and what we have forgotten. As such, it is seldom an accurate record of experience. I was recalling memories from my adolescence to a friend about a time I felt humiliated by my headteacher after missing a couple of 'O' level exams, without telling anyone, as I was anxious about my mother. I told my friend, '*That's why I walked out of school and never returned.*' I really did do that, but I now realise that was two and a half years after the event remembered. In my recall, the narrative memory had become conflated with one being the reason for the other.

If clients share explicit memories of traumatising experiences, coaches must be cautious about pressing for more information. The outcome can be unpredictable, and coaches are generally not equipped to work with it. We can listen attentively and empathically to what we are told and reflect on what we hear and observe. We can offer our clients a thought that maybe some of what they are experiencing in the 'here and now' has some connection with the 'there and then'. They may respond with the following or similar responses, which open up areas for exploration:

> '*I had never thought there might be any connection.*'

> '*I hadn't realised that the "there and then" could have such an impact on the "here and now".*'

Alternatively, clients may respond in a totally different way:

> *'No, I don't think there is any connection.'*

> *'No, I don't think that had much impact on me.'*

Responses like these likely indicate it is not something the client is prepared to explore. We might respond, for example, with: '*It seems quite an experience to have had and for some I imagine one that had a lasting effect.*' However, if the client does not pick up on this, it not for us to continue unless we have the client's permission.

There was a lot in the press some years ago about 'false memory' and 'false memory syndrome'. False memory relates to ideas that have been implanted in people about events that did not happen to them, or narratives that are created and falsely treated as memory. The original accusation was that therapists were implanting or creating false memories in their clients. Most accounts of so-called 'false memory' concerned sexual abuse. This is not something I think coaching needs to be concerned with. We must respect what our clients tell us, and it is not for us to decide whether we think it is true or not. It is also not our place to use techniques or use interventions to prompt the creation of narratives about the past to account for what is happening in the 'here and now'.

Even though explicit memory is open to distortion, that does not make it 'false memory', just incomplete memory. Only implicit memory, with its feelings and felt-body responses, leaves no doubt about the depth and reality of the felt experience.

It helps to differentiate between memory and narrative. While narrative is informed by memory, it becomes something else in the telling. The more it is told, the more the narrative shifts and the 'memory' can once more become distorted. My example of 'walking out of school' is a narrative. This is often what we hear in taking an autobiography. As such, it is open to exploration with clients if they wish to do so. We can invite them to look at what they were told happened and what they can directly remember, if anything. When I reflected on my narrative, I realised that what had been missed out of my conflated narrative was what had led me to walk out of school, never to return. This was interesting to reflect on and doing so provided insight about issues in the 'here and now'.

Bio-physiology and epigenetics

There is a developing scientific understanding of the impact of toxic (trauma) stress on the physiological and cellular structures within the body. The effect of these changes is reversible and new process can be created if the conditions are changed externally and internally, through doing personal work. The impact of trauma is therefore at a cellular level, hence the idea that there is a cellular memory – a part of implicit memory.

The body is made up of a complex network of systems transmitting and sharing information and energy. The chemicals needed for this transmission can be affected by trauma. For example, the production of serotonin can be distorted by the trauma response. Serotonin is a chemical that has a wide variety of functions in the human body, including its important contribution to well-being and the capacity for happiness. Some medical-trauma therapists include rebalancing elements of the chemicals as part of trauma healing. Other elements include developing the capacity for stress regulation and bringing implicit memory into conscious awareness through body-based therapies.

There is currently a debate within epigenetics – the study of inheritable changes that affect how cells read our genes – as to whether trauma stimulates such changes, which are then passed on from one generation to the next. Thus, my grandmother's trauma might have resulted in epigenetic modifications affecting how the genes are read within cellular structures that she passed on to my mother, and were then passed on to me, affecting my physiology. Although there is some evidence to suggest that this does occur, further research is required to confirm this. If an individual with trauma symptoms, such as violent or addicted survival behaviour, says '*It's in my genes*', they are displaying a victim mentality and are avoiding responsibility for changing their cellular structure and physiology by not engaging in personal work that uploads new information and energy into their systems.

The bio-physiology of trauma is a fascinating area for those interested in the science and helps us understand the depth and extent of the lasting impact of trauma. However, at present it doesn't change how we respond to trauma symptoms in the coaching process. For this reason, I have not addressed in detail this scientific aspect of the internalisation of trauma.

The impact on our sense of ourselves and our mental models of the world

Our earliest relationships are the basis for our sense of ourselves and our attachment patterns, which we carry with us into adult life. As I have already stated, the quality of the primary relationship between infants and their primary caregivers is crucial to our ideas about how lovable we are, how safe the world is, how much we can trust in others, and our capacity for self-compassion. Traumatised parents, who carry their own toxic stress and insecure attachment patterns, are unable to bond healthily with their children much of the time. Mothers and primary caregivers who do not feel lovable, safe or are able to trust easily pass this on to their infants through the dysfunctional bonding process.

Since human infants are totally dependent on others for their survival, they are very sensitive to signs of emotional distancing. They do whatever they can to entice their mother or others to care for them. These adaptive patterns of relating play out through later relationships with self, others, and with work. Gabor Maté (2013) talks of our choosing survival attachment over autonomy – that is, our freedom to be fully ourselves. This is also a common pattern in adulthood. We betray our own needs to meet the actual, perceived or projected needs of others.

Children who experienced secure attachment through having their dependency and development needs predictably and lovingly met grow into self-confident adults who can have healthy relationships, manage their boundaries, and make good choices for themselves. Children of parents who are traumatised develop insecure attachment patterns (Ainsworth et al., 1979), which they carry over into adult life. Any sense of safety, trust, and self-confidence is compromised, as are our ideas about ourselves, leading to a range of adaptive behaviours. We meet these ways of relating in coaching, in ourselves and in our clients. They are complex and deeply entrenched, as they have arisen from our earliest experience.

Psyche-trauma autobiography

Psyche-trauma is cumulative. Repeated traumatising experiences in early life produce a build-up of stress hormones and dissociative responses that are imprinted in our developing brain, neuropathways, and physiology. It is the building up, layer upon layer, of trauma responses. A *trauma biography*, the history of our trauma responses, is developed from the following experiences:

Early trauma	Not being wanted, complications with pregnancy, attempted abortion, toxic stress, and trauma experienced by the mother. In adulthood, may be prone to hypervigilance and anxiety; will have insecure attachment and issues about identity and self-worth.
Dysfunctional attachment	Not loved/feeling loved. Unpredictable meeting of symbiotic needs of infants; separation from mother, neglect. In adulthood, insecure attachment patterns, unsatisfying relationships, diminished stress regulation, low self-worth and self-confidence.
Physical and sexual abuse	Not protected. Betrayal on the part of those trusted and expected to protect us. In adulthood, confusion about love and abuse; difficulty recognising perpetrators for what they are; poor personal boundary management, and vulnerability to further abuse.

Where there is early trauma, it is most likely that there will also be trauma as a result of dysfunctional attachment. Individuals with early trauma and dysfunctional attachment are vulnerable to additional sexual and physical abuse. Those trauma-tised cumulatively in this way may also then become the perpetrators of abuse, which itself is traumatising, thus adding to the trauma biography (Ruppert, 2016).

People with a large trauma biography are likely to have disorganised and chaotic attachment patterns. They are more likely to suffer from alcohol and drug misuse and/or mental health problems, including depression, dissociative identity disor-der, and bipolar diagnoses. The extent of the trauma biography will have an impact on how effective coaching can be and what the impact on the coach will be.

In cases of sexual and/or physical abuse, children have been betrayed by those who are supposed to protect them. In most cases, such abuse is within bonded relationship networks such as families and small communities. Children who are abused are told to keep the abuse secret, and are often ignored or disbelieved if they try to reveal it. Abused children grow into adults who confuse love with abuse. As they are unable to recognise perpetrators, they often invite them into their lives. They are unable to protect their own boundaries or to leave a relationship that brings them harm. This means they can go from one abusive relationship to another, including at work.

Such children often become parents who are less able to protect themselves or their children. Their ego-boundaries are damaged and their frontal lobe is under-developed, making executive decision-making difficult. And they may find them-selves in abusive or unsupportive relationships as a result. The children of such parents are therefore vulnerable to neglect, physical and/or sexual abuse within the family or close community.

Sometimes a client will tell you about violence in the family, or sexual abuse, and dismiss it as not having really affected them, or that they have 'dealt with it'. It is not for coaches to contradict them but hold open the possibility that some of what they are dealing with in the 'here and now' is creating echoes of the 'there and then'. We cannot just 'deal' with something like this. However, a client may not want to discuss it all in coaching, as the pain of opening it up is too great or because it feels the wrong place for them to disclose it. Again, we must respect that; it is not our role to ask clients to open that memory file. We only need to acknowledge with the client that it exists.

Children born into poverty are born into a high stress environment, particularly if this includes malnourishment and lack of warmth. Not only does this affect their nutrition, physical and cognitive development, it is also likely that the main caregiv-ers are unable to attend sensitively to them because of the stress they themselves are under. For those readers wanting to understand the impact of traumatising poverty environments on children and adults, I recommend *Poverty Safari* (2017) by Darren McGarvey. He talks lucidly about dissociation and how switching off is used as a defence mechanism. He also describes the hypervigilance that becomes the default position in the event of unpredictable behaviour on the part of the parents/caregivers, as children cannot feel safe at home, yet have nowhere else to go. While this is a complex situation, there are similarities to children's responses within families where there are traumatising relationships of a less violent and unpredictable nature.

Our ideas about ourselves are formed in relationships with our early caregivers, along with our sense of self-worth and self-confidence, and our capacity for self-compassion. We can help clients make a link between their sense of themselves and their attachment patterns with their history, if we have enough information from the client's autobiography.

> '*K, I wonder if how you feel about your boss has any connection with your experience as a child with either of your parents?*'

> '*Our early relationships as young children have a lasting impact on how we relate to people as adults. What connections, if any, can you see between what you are talking about with work colleagues, and what happened to you as a child?*'

Different parenting structures

I realise that the picture I am presenting is of a traditional form of conceiving and giving birth. There is another conversation about the traumatised psyche where the gestational mother is not the same as the person raising the child, for example through surrogacy, using a donated egg or IVF, or adoption and fostering. The changes to the process of conception bring another dimension to thinking about the psyche and brain development. Surrogacy will have the same impact on the infant as that for other adoptions. Adoption is a psyche-trauma for the infant. However, the post adoption environment can be one where infants feel protected and loved. The additional impact on attachment will depend on how traumatised the adoptive parents are and how this affects their responses to the needs of the infant. Fostering often brings about repeated change and insecurity, affecting attachment capability.

Listening to client narratives

Coaches hear client narratives frequently, particularly when we ask for autobiographical information and as clients make links with 'there and then' in relation to 'here and now'. If clients share experiences that are distressing to them, we just need to listen, be a witness to the story, and validate their feelings. We do not need to rescue them from the distress or rescue ourselves by moving the client on quickly.

If clients share their memories of traumatising experiences, we can ask questions such as the following:

> '*How are you right now talking about this?*'

> '*How did you survive? What resources did you use?*'

'*How is this experience affecting you today in your day-to-day functioning?*'

'*In what ways might this affect the work we are doing, if at all?*'

'*What else might I need to know for our coaching work to be effective?*'

'*What, if any, professional help are you getting or have you had around these issues?*'

If clients talk a lot about the past and the coaching is not progressing, it is possible that they are using the past as a distraction or a way of not attending to the present. We can all get caught up in retelling the same stories about our past as a means of avoiding what is going on in the 'here and now'. In supervision, I often hear from coaches who are frustrated because their clients keep talking about something 'out there' which seems to avoid connecting with the reality of their present. If this is starting to happen, bring clients into the present by asking them, '*How does this connect, if at all, with what is happening currently for you?*' Or use other coaching interventions to interrupt the story-telling.

The use of autobiography in coaching is information-gathering not diagnostic. We can, however, listen out for indications of traumatising experiences, which we can then use later in the coaching to make links between 'there and then' and 'here and now'. It is the survival defences to that experience which have the negative impact on life in the 'here and now'. Examples of things we can listen out for include:

Stories about the pregnancy and its context, which indicate the child may not have been wanted or was the result of rape; maternal or infant difficulties during pregnancy; being the sole survivor of twins.	Caesarean or difficult births; the need for care in an incubator, or early surgery.
Any separation from the mother early in life, including death, hospitalisation of mother or client, adoption, or fostering.	Death of either parent or close attachment figures early in life without adequate emotional support. Being sent to boarding school at a young age.
Parents who were addicted to alcohol, prescribed or illegal drugs.	Physical violence in the home directed at the child – or that the child heard, saw or sensed – on a regular basis.
Sexual abuse as a child or violent rape at a later age.	Sibling bullying and abuse, including sexual abuse.

An older or younger sibling who required a lot of attention from the mother and others due to disability, serious illness or death. This includes a stillbirth prior to the client being conceived.	The child became a carer to the mother, from a young age and for a long time, due to mother's illness or disability.
Extreme poverty.	Big memory gaps – these can be a symptom of dissociation in childhood.
Being conceived, being in utero or born into a war zone or where threat levels were very high.	Parents caught up in a war or armed conflict, as combatants or civilians, prior to conception.
Narratives about parenting styles that were controlling, without boundaries, critical, cold, inconsistent, smothering, or rejecting; expectations that felt unreasonable.	Stories of the parents wanting a child of the opposite sex, or of the birth being 'inconvenient' in some other way.

It is also helpful when gathering autobiographical information to use techniques that get away from the well-rehearsed narratives and provide more of an insight into the inner dynamics of the child. Such approaches might use questions, for example, around what characters in books, television programmes or films the

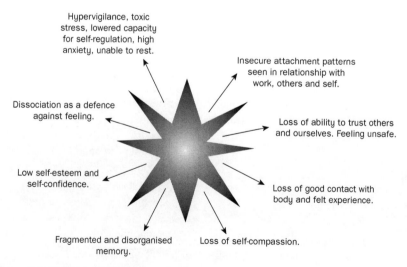

Figure 2.2 The impact of trauma

client identified with, what stories/films they enjoyed and why, and what imaginary games they created for themselves. This gives a different insight into ideas about themselves and who they identified with, and why.

The lasting impact of such experience creates trauma shadows from the past into the present (see Figure 2.2).

Neuroplasticity

For decades it was thought that the brain was immutable, unchangeable, and static. New research in the field of neuroscience has shown this core belief to be incorrect and that the brain is, in fact, a dynamic organ that changes constantly.

As neuroscience and biology research develop, it is clear that the brain can reorganize itself by forming new neural connections throughout life. Neuroplasticity allows the neurones – the nerve cells – in the brain to compensate for injury and disease and to adjust their activity in response to new situations or environmental changes.

Trauma healing involves releasing unconscious implicit memory through feeling connections with the body, referred to as embodied experience. Such re-experiencing enables our physiological systems to be involved and 'updated'. In this way, it is possible to move away from toxic stress and the impact of one's trauma biography, but first we must do the therapeutic work.

It is important to be aware of what in our history can have a traumatising impact on us. This helps us to face the reality of our experience and make connections with difficulties in the 'here and now'. It is not the role of coaching, however, to determine for clients what was traumatising for them or not. That must be for clients to explore and decide.

For coaches, understanding the factors in the early environment that might be traumatising is to appreciate that the 'here and now' may have deep roots in the past, meaning that the connections are well established. It can also be helpful for clients to make the connections for themselves, as it can bring valuable insight and a different way of thinking about the choices open to them as adults.

This chapter has only provided a very brief introduction to the neuroscience of attachment trauma and I hope this information will be of value. For those readers who would have liked more, I recommend the works of Allan Schore (2001, 2010), Gabor Maté (2003, 2013), Babette Rothschild (2000), and Bessel van der Kolk (2015).

3 A way of conceptualising trauma

I have been learning from Professor Franz Ruppert (www.franz-ruppert.de) over the last nine years. This chapter draws on his work and is a distilled account of his theory about trauma and his simple model for the complex process, which is very useful for coaching.

Ruppert's theory is readily accessible and can help coaches and clients cultivate self-awareness and enhance personal development. It helps us to understand why coaching might not be working, and the coach's part in that, and thus what action to take. To understand trauma in ourselves, we need to work personally with a suitably trained therapist. However, understanding the theory helps with our own self-reflective practice and supports effective coaching.

Ruppert's model – the split in the psyche

Ruppert's ideas of how trauma acts within us and the impact it has on our behaviour as children and adults in relationship with ourselves and others have been developed over twenty-five years of clinical practice and research. His work has led the way in identifying our vulnerability to trauma from conception onwards and how it presents in adults.

The point of the freeze, fragment, submission, and dissociation trauma response, Ruppert (2012, 2014, 2016) says, is to create a 'split in the psyche'. In order to withstand the painful emotions of the trauma, he talks of an emerging survival self, which functions to keep the trauma feelings isolated from our conscious awareness and creates a split in the wholeness of the psyche. This survival self is reinforced as life continues and by adulthood may be driving how someone lives their life. It acts as a defensive personality shield, ensuring the fragmented trauma feelings remain concealed.

One of the strengths of this model is that a healthy 'self' and 'parts' remain unaffected by trauma. The healthy self carries our unfragmented self and sense of who we are. It continues to carry the momentum of the quest for life, health, and *individuation,* meaning becoming fully ourselves. The extent of this part or self, and our capacity to access its resources, depends on our *trauma biography* – that is, our trauma history from birth onwards. Clients are often reassured that there is a healthy part and can recognise times when they felt in contact with it.

Figure 3.1 illustrates the three elements of the split: the trauma self, survival self, and healthy self. The size of these 'selves' will be different for each of us, depending

Figure 3.1 The split in the psyche

Source: © 2012 Franz Ruppert.

on our trauma biography. The proportions for each individual can also change in response to the adult's environment. For example, if the work or personal environment in the 'here and now' mimics aspects of the 'there and then', the trauma self and survival self will be enlarged, and the healthy self will be reduced. This is why some organisations, roles, and relationships have a negative impact on us.

The healthy self

The healthy self carries the sense of ourselves unaffected by trauma. There is a steady flow of information and energy between emotions, body, and mind. The healthy self is without heightened stress and anxiety, enabling us to think clearly and face the truth, however painful. There is a good connection with emotions and the body. We have self-compassion and self-worth.

We can understand this as a functioning right hemisphere, communicating effectively with the left hemisphere, together with a functioning connection between the frontal lobe, limbic system, and brain stem. The healthy self has feelings – maybe sadness, anger, grief, shame – all of which are normal responses to external factors. However, we are not overwhelmed or consumed by them. Importantly, we can also feel love, joy, and passion within this self, feelings that are unavailable to us in the other selves.

It is the place where we have contact with our sense of agency. That is, the sense that our life is ours to live and to direct, and thus provides the capacity to take the actions we need. We are not waiting for, or making, others decide for us;

nor are we avoiding life decisions. It is the capacity to connect with our 'will' rather than will power. We know what we need to be healthy; we can distinguish what is healthy from what is not.

Ruppert (2012) uses the term *healthy autonomy* to describe relating to others from the healthy self. We can be close to others while not compromising our needs, and without adapting to the needs of others. As we are no longer afraid of rejection or feeling alone, we can remove ourselves from relationships that are unhealthy for us. Unhealthy relationships may demand we become a different person, or must compromise our needs too much, or that we continually have to meet the demands of the other. Removing ourselves healthily means we don't have to resort to rebellion, or revenge, control, or rescuing, all of which are parts of the survival self.

The healthy self is where personal insight and change is possible. It is the important ingredient for coaching, for both coaches and clients.

The trauma self

The trauma self carries the emotional pain and fragmented memory of the traumatising events. Thinking '*it's a good thing to keep the pain well hidden*', which unfortunately many of us were told, doesn't make for a healthy psyche. It is the cut-off nature of the emotions together with the predominance of the survival self that creates problems in adult life. The emotions associated with the trauma derive in part from not having our physical and developmental needs met, being abandoned or being the victim of abuse. They are feelings of terror, rage, intense loneliness, a profound lack of safety, shame, and emotional distress. While they remain concealed, they nonetheless have a continuous impact on us in the 'here and now'.

These feelings are frozen at the time of the original dissociation. They do not 'mature' with the growing child/adult but remain associated with the age at which they were experienced. Hence, if they erupt, there is a regression, and we become the age of the child at which the feelings were experienced. Such re-experiencing can be accompanied by shaking or feeling cold. Some of the memories will be from before we had language, and while we feel the effect, we are not necessarily able to express them as emotions we can name. We may fear being overwhelmed by remembering, or that we might fragment, or in some way be destroyed. The survival self's function is to stop us remembering the feelings.

We occasionally meet the trauma self in coaching, although rarely. *Re-traumatisation* is the term used for when the 'here and now' triggers the trauma feelings from the 'there and then'.

The survival self

The purpose of the survival self is to block out the trauma feelings. It is a complex defence system that involves survival strategies, the creation of an adapted identity, and ways of managing relationships, all in an attempt to keep perceived danger away.

The survival self involves a loss of connection with our bodies, which means we are less able to connect with our felt experience – that is, our emotions, sensations, gut feelings – in the 'here and now'. Instead, we create a range of cognitive and behavioural survival strategies. Survival involves high levels of stress that come to feel the norm.

In Chapter 2, I referred to dissociation, which can be a survival defence response of both clients and coaches. When a coach becomes dissociated, they 'go through the motions' without really 'seeing' or engaging with the client.

Coaching is enhanced the more able coaches are to remain attuned to their body, and thus remain fully present in their healthy self. If you sense you have 'gone somewhere else' or are 'just in your head', focus on grounding yourself. That is, breathe deeply, feel your feet firmly on the ground and your bottom firmly on the chair. Reconnect with your environment.

Dissociation is a survival defence response to an activation of 'there and then' memories from the 'here and now'. It also accounts for memory gaps in the autobiography. Other survival defences include denial, illusion, addictions, distractions, control of self and others, rescuing, avoidance, mental illness, and *somatisation* – the expression of emotional distress through physical symptoms.

Denial is a powerful defence. It involves refusing to accept something that part of us knows to be true. The unconscious motivation is to deny our trauma. It can be seen in clients who deny any emotional impact from a potentially traumatising experience. In the example below, the client is in denial about his father but recognises some response to his current boss. As he talks, the client is not making the connection because of denial:

> *'He, my boss, reminds me of my father when he was ranting and violent at home. Even though my father didn't affect me because I left the house when I could. This guy does bother me though.'*

While the survival strategies, such as denial, aim to keep the trauma pain suppressed, the trauma feelings are not inactive. They continue to influence our behaviour and sense of well-being and imprison us in the past. However, it is not for coaches to push for trauma feelings or memory. That is not our function and could be damaging for the client.

I recently experienced denial myself and was shocked by how powerful it was. I felt fit and healthy, was running 8K regularly, when I was told I needed an emergency heart operation. In fact, I was admitted directly into hospital and was told that I was lucky not to be dead already. The survival part of me refused to believe there was a problem with my heart, even though I had been a nurse, or that I was at risk, despite the ECG evidence in front of me, and a consultant had to tell me at least three times while looking me straight in the eye. I was convinced they were wrong. When I reflected, I realised that part of me had known for months that something was wrong, as I had had occasional chest pain. My healthy part had taken me to the doctor. However, the survival part flipped into denial. From that place, I tried to get the doctor to collude with my diagnosis that the symptoms were grief-stress related. I recognised my survival strategy as a pattern at different stages in my life, when I was facing something very serious. Facing the truth means I must make big adjustments in my sense of myself and allow vulnerability and fear to be present.

Coaches often hear indications of denial:

> '*I am fine, just a bit tired.*'

> '*I like working very hard.*'

> '*Nothing happened to me.*'

> '*Everything was very happy at home.*'

> '*Well, boarding school wasn't great, but it was also fine, I'm sure it did me good.*'

> '*No need to slow down – I can keep going.*'

> '*My headaches are a nuisance, but I keep taking the painkillers – it's not a problem.*'

We can detect denial if what is said contradicts other things the client tells us. For example, if explored, '*I am fine, just tired*' may actually mean that the client is exhausted and has been for a long time. If it is a temporary state, then while there is some denial, in that the '*I am fine*' bit sounds more like reassurance than a reality, it is a passing phase. In the boarding school example, the conflicting story is in the phrase. We can enquire in what way being at boarding school might have some connection with the issues being explored in coaching. In this way, we are not arguing with the client but opening up what is closed down by the denial.

Accepting the truth means we have some major adjustments to make, as I did myself. The survival strategy of illusion is closely related to that of denial. Denial can create illusions about our experience and ideas. People sometimes talk of wanting to be free, but when explored, that idea of 'being free' is an illusion of some perfect, all-loving place without the problems of personal interaction. Some forms of engagement with spirituality can also be illusory, such as when they carry ideas of perfection or release from the human condition. It is when spirituality is engaged with from the survival self that it becomes an illusion. It is then being used as an attempt to bypass the work needed for emotional integration. This is also the case when we create idealised ideas of the future or of others. I have been in the audience of a motivational speaker several times, hearing him talk of the deep spiritual journey he made and how that led him to a compassionate and caring approach to leadership. The audiences were always motivated and wanted to jump straight to becoming that sort of leader and learn quickly from him. What they forgot was him saying that he had spent twenty-one years in his earlier adulthood meditating and learning with mentors in a structured way.

The best place to start with the idea of illusion as defence is with ourselves. Are we using illusion to avoid dealing with something important? When we hear clients talk of what we think of as an illusion in their narrative, an appropriately offered challenge may sometimes be useful. However, a client may not be able to take this in and we can hold the observation for a time when they might be more receptive. Positive thinking can also be included under the heading of illusion, when it is used to escape from reality. Similarly, naming feelings as 'good' or 'bad' is to misunderstand their function, especially if 'bad' feelings then must be banished. All feelings need to be welcome and accommodated, to see what they can tell us. We need not become overwhelmed by them or act them out. Although there is much of value in positive thinking, we need to be mindful of its potential misuse as a survival strategy. The opposite of illusory positive thinking isn't negative thinking; it is the ability to engage with reality from the healthy self.

The toxic stress associated with trauma brings a range of distressing emotions with it and survival strategies, such as addiction, seek to numb this distress. Addiction can relate to alcohol, exercise, overwork, sex, shopping, drugs, social media/internet use, or gambling. Addictions offer a moment of escape, a 'high' of some sort, but then a low as the high fades rapidly. We reach for another glass of wine to 'relax us' or 'unwind us', when we all know that it doesn't, and then, when that stops providing the comfort we seek, we increase the amount we drink. Or individuals take analgesics regularly for headaches or other pains. In extreme cases, people reach for illegal drugs or so-called legal 'highs'. Some use excessive consumerism to numb distress. Some people shop for things they never wear or use. Working obsessively blocks out uncomfortable emotions or issues about relating to ourselves and others. Clients who have work–life balance problems that coaching doesn't resolve are likely to be using work in this way. A useful book for understanding addictions is *In the Realm of the Hungry Ghosts* (2013), by Gabor Maté, based on his many years working with drug addicts in Canada.

Distraction is part of addiction and serves to remove us from what we are feeling. Distraction is anything that takes our mind and attention away from the feeling. Rushing around cleaning the house before leaving on holiday may be a distraction, for example, from the anxiety connected with flying. Clients use distraction from feelings when they talk about things 'out there' to stop the coach focusing on what is 'in here' in the 'here and now'. They may relate long narratives without expressing any emotion or talk about other people. Coaches use distraction when they introduce another tool or exercise to relieve them from anxiety or get caught up in their own helplessness with clients they find 'difficult'.

We also manage our inner distress and anxiety through control of ourselves, others, and our environment. Control of ourselves might be about our appearance, food intake, exercise or belongings, what we allow ourselves to do and make us not do. It stops any spontaneity. We control others by telling them what they can and can't to, by setting limits on them and punishing them when they don't comply. Controlling others enables us to feel 'in charge' and invulnerable to others' whims or needs. Control is a form of perpetration. By using control, we try to calm the internal disorder. We avoid inconvenience as much as possible, to create an illusion of being in control. As a result, we can imprison ourselves.

Our relationship with food can be a problem. This might be through binge eating, which involves eating normally but, when emotionally triggered, eating so much that it hurts and might result in vomiting. For others, forms of self-starvation or food deprivation, or vomiting after eating, is a means of controlling and suppressing painful emotion. For some, the complex relationship with food might take on less extreme behaviour. These are all survival strategies, arising from trauma, using a combination of addiction, denial, control, and self-harm. Coaching clients rarely talk about their relationship with food and working with those who have such survival responses requires specialist skills. However, such behaviour is a sign of trauma, and if talked about we can listen, enquire, and support the client find the help they need. This survival behaviour is unlikely to be the only strategy clients use to keep trauma distress suppressed.

Rescuing and seeing oneself as a victim of others, when this isn't the case, are also survival strategies. They are responses to relationships that have some connection with 'there and then'. Compensation, for example clownish behaviour, is another survival strategy. This includes being the entertainer, cracking jokes, and laughing on the verge of hysteria. It can be helpful to feed back to clients your observations of such behaviour and invite them to speculate what might lie behind it. For example:

> '*I notice that you are talking about rescuing people a lot at work and that you end up taking on more work. I wonder what you think that might be about?*'

> '*I notice you are a joker, and that you said you were the clown at school and do that now; and yet you are concerned that you are not always seen as a serious contender for promotion. I wonder what you think being the clown is about?*'

Since the survival strategies emerge from traumatising relationships, our surviving self is cautious and conflicted about close relationships. Healthy intimacy needs the healthy self to relate to another healthy self. From the survival self we repeat the entangled relationship of early life; consequently, relationships with others and with work suffer.

Karen Horney (1950) identified a relational defence system before there was any real understanding of the impact of relational trauma. Horney linked the idea of identity with self-hatred, which we now understand to be an internalisation of the hatred or lack of loving attunement we felt in early relationships. She hypothesised that we carry this self-loathing over into our behaviour. Recent work on attachment and trauma means that we interpret the behaviour she observed differently now, although the three categories she identified remain helpful to our understanding. She described 'moving towards', 'moving away from', and 'moving against' as relational choices.

- *Moving towards*: seeking approval, reassurance, clinging dependency, and being compliant. This arises from doubting our own worth and involves wanting the 'other' to rescue us.
- *Moving away from*: withdrawing from real contact. It often includes a need for perfection, which is an illusion. Individuals seek independence so as not to have to rely on others, and risk being hurt by them. As a result, life and aspirations become limited through deep feelings, from the 'there and then', of being threatened and undeserving.
- *Moving against*: an aggressive form of relating, using power and exploitation as substitutes for contact and intimacy.

Note the links with insecure attachment patterns. We take our earliest experience of relationship as a framework for future relationships with ourselves, others, and with work.

The body is always present when the mind might be elsewhere. So, even if we are not consciously experiencing some thing or other, the body is. We might adopt certain postures as a way of surviving a traumatising experience, which can lead to muscular and skeletal issues in adulthood. For example, I am troubled by shoulder pain, some of which can be explained by sitting too long at a computer desk, but I have come to recognise that it is also connected to how I hold my body when I am tense. It is a physical pattern of holding myself in a stressed state from the 'there and then'. As well as the body taking on particular positions, the toxic stress of trauma causes headaches, gut problems such as irritable bowel syndrome, autoimmune and endocrine disorders. These arise from the stress hormones acting on these physiological systems. The medical doctor and therapist, Gabor Maté, talks about the body's response to the toxic stress of trauma in his book *When the Body Says No* (2003). He provides examples of patients who may say 'it's only stress' and avoid any medical examination. This is both denial of actual physical ailments, which might be serious, as my heart condition was, and the exacerbation of them through continuing with a work addiction. The connection of toxic stress and body systems is also set out in Ruppert and Banzhaf (2018). We may meet clients who tell us they work very hard and long hours, with a work addiction, and that they have a problem with their gut but who see no connection between the two. The body can only take so much toxic stress.

It is well documented that people can become ill, be in pain or even become disabled where there is no identifiable physical cause. The consultant neurologist

Dr Suzanne O'Sullivan describes some of these more extreme examples in her book *It's All in Your Head* (2015). She presents case studies of patients who, for instance, appeared to be in the grip of epileptic seizures but in fact were not, or who became so immobile that they needed constant care and a wheelchair, yet there was no diagnosable physical cause. She makes the point that although there was no underlying physical problem, these patients were genuinely ill; their bodies had taken over from their minds and were mimicking the symptoms experienced. Such individuals are likely to continue looking for a diagnosis and treatment, without relief. Through the impact of trauma on the connection with the body, many will feel their vulnerability physically and will often rely on external regulation or reassurance. For example, they may attend the doctor's surgery on a regular basis, or have anxieties about their health or the health of others.

Denial, distraction, addiction, and control can, as we have seen, lead us to ignore physical symptoms, often to the detriment of our well-being. How people treat and relate to their body has something to say about how we relate to others. Here is a coach talking about a client:

> '*I experience V as being very controlled and controlling. She is good at her job but she seems to see her body as a machine to enable her to work. When she talks about others at work she has no empathy or compassion for those around her who are tired or ill, or disabled. She seems to treat them as if they are of no value if they are not working intensely. She is having problems with them for being what she describes as feeble.*'

This client treats her body and those of others as machines. It makes leadership impossible as people dislike such treatment. The issue is her relationship with her body. The expression of emotional distress through physical symptoms, referred to as somatisation, is not something coaches are well equipped to deal with, unless they have proper training in body-based working. However, they have available to them the interventions of observation and feedback. If clients are unable to have self-compassion or self-care, you can intervene and encourage clients to take their bodies seriously. You can explain the links between stress and sleep or gut problems and offer coaching to help clients find solutions that might be healthy for them. Importantly, you can focus on yourself and reflect on your own attitude to your body and your own body armour. In the next chapter, I talk a bit more about encouraging clients to connect with their bodily felt experience.

Another set of survival strategies are those labelled 'mental health problems'. Such diagnoses include depression, bipolar disorder, psychosis, obsessive compulsive disorder, hoarding, anorexia, bulimia, personality, and anxiety disorders. These diagnostic categories have been created to bring together symptoms and to help mental health professionals make a diagnosis and prescribe treatment. The evidence for the success of treatments is variable and many of the symptoms become chronic, that is long-lasting and a core factor in a person's life. These conditions are a complex combination of emotional, physiological, and cognitive associated with trauma.

The survival self's presence in coaching

The selves we mostly meet in both ourselves and our clients are the healthy self and the survival self (Figures 3.2 and 3.3). When coaching is not flowing smoothly, then you can be sure that clients are in their survival self and that you probably are too. The more pronounced the survival self in terms of use of the survival strategies, the greater the activation of the trauma feelings beneath the surface. The enhanced survival strategies are needed to keep them hidden.

It is the adaptive behaviour of the survival self that causes the problems for us and those around us. It is not the pain of the trauma itself, although significant, but our fear and denial of it. As long as the trauma is unresolved, and the trauma feelings remain cut off, the stress hormones are always on high alert, leaving the person fighting unseen dangers. The work to enable the integration of trauma feelings and reality is the work of therapy, not of coaching. However, coaching can help clients enhance their capacity for accessing the resources in the healthy self and becoming self-aware of their survival strategies.

Where a mother, father or partner is traumatised, they will use their survival strategies and insecure attachment patterns when relating to their children. This

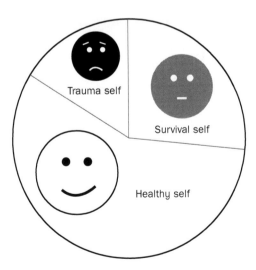

Figure 3.2 Predominantly healthy self

Source: Adapted from Vivian Broughton (2014).

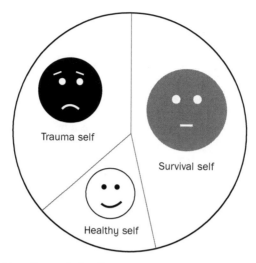

Figure 3.3 Predominantly survival self

Source: Adapted from Vivian Broughton (2014).

results in non-attunement and dysfunctional attachment. The survival strategies used will include controlling infants and objectifying them so as not to have to relate to them as people in their own right. They may also carry the illusion that having a baby *'will make everything all right'*. There will be dissociation, denial, and avoidance.

Parents have a healthy self from which they can attune to their infant and manage their own anxieties and feelings that arise in relation to the dependence of the infant. It is the inconsistency and unpredictability of the move from survival to healthy parenting that is traumatising to the infant. Some parents are so traumatised that there is not much of a healthy self to connect with the young child.

In suppressing the trauma feelings, survival strategies are exhausting and remove the capacity for spontaneity. They all carry a driven element. Often any attempt to shift them is rebuffed:

> *'No, you don't understand . . . I have to attend to all this before I do X.'*

> *'No, I'm not overworking but I just have to get on top of everything, as there is so much to do.'*

You can hold open the contradiction that the client presents, in wanting to change yet resisting changing their behaviour. An enquiry, as below, has to come from

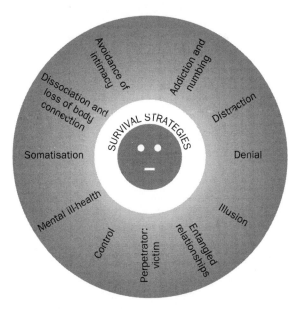

Figure 3.4 Survival strategies

your healthy space and be within the context of a good working alliance with the client, one where trust and safety have been established:

> '*I see you as being exhausted by work, using up all your energy so you have no space for what you say you enjoy. I imagine, though, that you see yourself as doing what has to be done, of ensuring you are keeping on the leading edge of things. I wonder if, at some level, you are afraid that you may not be kept on at work if you don't do this?*'

This is aimed at the healthy self. Figure 3.4 summarises the survival strategies.

Trauma biography

The trauma biography is our trauma history. In Ruppert's model, each traumatising experience sees another split to the psyche, resulting in further internal fragmentation. This is like having many distorted and fragmented mirrors within us (Kalsched, 2013). As a result, people with the most extensive trauma biography are often far less able to manage their lives and relationships and therefore less likely to come into the coaching process.

There is no statistical evidence to illustrate the prevalence of trauma within society, or the proportions of traumatised individuals who have an 'extensive' or 'less extensive' trauma biography. However, we can assume that there is a spectrum, with those who have had cumulative trauma from dysfunctional attachment, sexual and physical abuse at one end, and those with less invasive and cumulative trauma at the other. In coaching, we rarely work with those with the most extensive trauma biographies, just as therapists rarely work with those who are not so deeply affected.

Ruppert (2014; Ruppert and Banzhaf, 2018) describes the progression of a trauma biography as follows:

- *Trauma of identity.* This, Ruppert states, results from early trauma and its impact on the psyche, the network of physiological, emotional, and neurological cells, and stress and dissociation in utero. The development of the healthy self is affected by this and consequent splits. The survival self comes into being. Knowing 'who we are' is about being in emotional connection with ourselves, having a defined identity description. Early trauma damages these connections between body, emotions, and thoughts. Trauma of identity relates to this loss of a deepening connection with ourselves. We therefore develop a replacement survival identity through the responses of our survival self to the environment.
- *Trauma of love.* This results from the dysfunctional attachment relationship with a traumatised mother or primary caregiver. It leads us into life-long entangled or co-dependent relationships with those around us. We search for love and belonging, or prevent any possibility of being loved so that it cannot be taken away from us. There is a core pain of loneliness and abandonment.
- *Trauma of sexuality.* Not only does this have a damaging effect on our sense of ourselves and our trust in others, it also has an impact on our sense and expression of our own sexuality.
- *Trauma of being a perpetrator.* Within this theory, all perpetrators have at one time been a victim with an extensive trauma biography. Acting as a perpetrator and harming others further splits the psyche.

Ruppert's therapeutic process

Ruppert has developed a therapeutic process through his clinical work that offers a way of bringing the unconscious splits in the psyche into conscious awareness using body-based experience. The split off trauma feelings can be felt safely, without becoming overwhelmed, allowing the healthy self to expand and the survival self to diminish. While this is a unique process, other trauma therapies – such as sensorimotor therapy and somatic experiencing – work with the same intention. All such therapies need specialist training and skill.

However, coaching can make a valuable contribution to trauma healing through the connections that can be made with the 'here and now' and the 'there and then', and with the feelings that underlie our survival responses. Our major contribution is to focus on the healthy self, and support clients to access and utilise those resources, rather than returning to the resources of the survival self. It is the resources in the healthy self that will take us to therapeutic work if we feel we need it.

Issues for coaching

How is this way of thinking about the trauma dynamics useful or relevant to coaching? The starting point must be with yourself, exploring your own survival strategies in general, and more specifically with clients. You can use this model as part of your reflective enquiry into your work. It might be particularly helpful to do this with a client you are not enjoying working with, finding it hard going, or feel ready to refer on. In what ways are you operating in survival mode? Are you distracting yourself and the client? Are they distracting you? Are you directing the coaching too much or sitting back feeling bored by the client's distraction or dissociation? Are you rescuing them or punishing them? What is at the root of your response? It is likely to be a core issue from the 'there and then'.

My main message to all coaches is that if we keep coaching from our healthy, grounded self, it doesn't matter what the trauma is within clients or how it is showing itself. This sounds easy but believe me it isn't. What happens instead is that we get caught up in the unconscious dynamic of our own and step into our survival self and strategies. As a result, we stop coaching. Staying grounded and in our own healthy self means that we are not applying our 'there and then' patterns with clients. Staying in the healthy self doesn't always result in a positive coaching outcome. That will depend on the amount of healthy self a client has available in coaching. However, it does mean that the coach will neither have responded from their survival self nor become consumed by negative thoughts about their own competence. Being in our healthy self means we can realistically think about our interventions with compassion and without self-criticism and learn from that process. Coaching is effective when coaches 'talk to' the healthy self of clients, from their own healthy self.

You don't need 'new tools' to work with trauma, you need to do your own development work to be able to stay in your healthy self most of the time when with a client. This is why this book is not a 'tool kit' for working with trauma. You can be most effective when you are fully present, feel grounded and attuned to the client; that way you can select and use interventions wisely and appropriately. All powerful open questions starting with 'How?', 'What?', 'Where?', 'Who?', 'When?' are aimed at the healthy part – closed questions are not, and neither are implied commands hidden as questions. You can ask open questions to involve the healthy self:

> '*I hear that a lot is going not well for you at the moment, but wondered what aspects of your life are going well?*'

> '*I hear you are uncertain about a lot of things, but what are you certain about?*'

'What is present, but you may not be facing?' (asked of a client who seems to be going round and round in their narrative)

'In what ways might it be possible that the pains you get reflect something you haven't been paying attention to?' (asked of a client who suffers with physical pains)

All of these and similar enquiries need to be asked where there is enough trust and safety, created through a good working alliance.

When we are in survival mode, coaches and clients are likely to enter silences too quickly. When asking such questions, give the healthy self time to respond; the survival self might jump in first but given space something else might be vocalised.

While it is important to recognise the potentially damaging impact of the split and the resulting survival strategies, it is important to recognise their purpose. They are an attempt to 'keep us safe' and from being overwhelmed by our vulnerability, that is, our painful emotions. They both prevent that contact while also preventing the integration of the feelings needed for recovery. Our function in coaching is not to try to 'break down' or attack the survival strategies of the client, but to acknowledge their presence with the client.

Although it is unlikely to be helpful explaining trauma biography to a client, it is worth explaining that different traumatising experiences build up within us from early in life. It is helpful to provide clients with an understanding that our early life experiences continue to influence our relational and work choices and behaviour in later life – that is, the 'there and then' influences the 'here and now'. If clients ask about what kinds of experiences, of course tell them.

Using Ruppert's model of the split self can be valuable as a way of helping clients understand what may be going on for them. However, it is very important that you completely understand it, have thought about it in relation to yourself, and practised introducing it – for example, in peer supervision.

Introducing Ruppert's model to clients is the same as introducing any model or tool. First, seek the client's permission for its use by telling them how it may be of benefit to the work they are doing in coaching. In talking about the three selves, start with, and emphasise, the healthy self. With the survival self, pick up those strategies that you may have observed the client using. You can also talk of how widespread such trauma is in the population and normalise its presence in individuals. In that way, the client can see it is part of the human condition. While their own experience is unique, similar experiences are replicated widely across the population.

Case example 3.1

'The client, a senior executive, was coming about work-related issues to do with how she was experienced in her role; however, she had also suffered burnout and had to take time off work. When I asked about her biographical information in the first session, she said she had suffered

long periods of separation from the family as a young child as her mother had become mentally ill and had periods of hospitalisation. Her parents divorced after a difficult relationship when she was nine, and her father later remarried and had another family. Her mother died when the client was thirteen.'

This is a good example of potentially traumatising experience. We don't know about her gestational and early years, but we see a pattern of potential traumatisation and re-traumatisation having a significant impact on the client and her ways of surviving them.

'The issues the client was coming to coaching for included feeling under great pressure at work, recognising that she had problems with relationships and recognising that she was what she called an almost compulsive runner, running at 5 am every morning for over an hour, and using caffeine to keep her going. It all became too much for her and she had to take time off work as she was on the edge of collapse. Her body was suffering from over-exercise, lack of rest, and high stress responses. She had also become very lonely and depressed.

*'I think she is coming to help resource her healthy self. After the first session I sent her the model and she said that it resonated with her. It transpired that she had read some books on trauma a few years ago and made the links from that reading to the model and to the work in hand. I want to support her healthy self and explore with her **whether her current role and organisation can be part of a healthy future for her**, so that she can put down some of the survival behaviour that she is wanting to stop and can step into her own healthy autonomy and authority.'*

We see here a range of survival strategies which exhausted her in her attempt to 'keep going' and to keep the painful feelings at bay. The coach's comment in bold above is supporting the client in using the resources of her healthy self.

Case example 3.2

'The client is a real high achiever, but she said she recognised that she was exhausted and the pace at which she was working did not feel sustainable. Her work pattern had badly affected her relationships outside work. Some days she said she felt despair at being on this 'hamster-wheel' as she called it but felt compelled to continue.

'She said she had big memory gaps about the early years; that there had been some complications at her birth but had never enquired what. She described her parents as cold, distant, and demanding.'

There isn't much autobiographical information on this client, although the memory gaps suggest, perhaps, periods of dissociation. However, we can hypothesise that the environment was traumatising. The complications of birth may mean that mother and baby were in a 'life and death' struggle, or that the mother suffered problems that meant she wasn't available to her newborn, or that the client as a baby was affected.

> *'On the third session, when not much had changed, I introduced the model to her. I felt it might help her self-awareness. We talked of over-work being like an addiction and a survival response. She 'got it' and shared that she had suffered anorexia in her early adulthood. We talked about the 'there and then' in the trauma feelings being reactivated and survival strategies responding. She then talked of her fear of not being good enough and of being punished for being lazy, which she immediately linked with the 'there and then'. When she returned for the fourth session, she said she had reflected a lot on our conversation. She said she felt that she couldn't reduce this survival response in her current work context and had been thinking about what might be healthier for her.'*

This, too, is about looking how to use the resources in the healthy self rather than relying on the resources in the survival self, which challenge our health and well-being.

Case example 3.3

> *'The client was having some relational problems at work. He seemed to need to be in control and was controlling of himself. It seemed as if he just wanted everyone else to change and yet could see that his behaviour was unhelpful.*
>
> *'I introduced this model to my client on the third session as I thought his contact with the healthy self was limited and we were not making much progress. He had talked about problems as a child, but very non-specifically. He said his sister was born with a disability and needed a lot of attention. I think she was eighteen months younger than him but am not sure. I felt he didn't want to talk about it at all. I got the sense that there was a lot of disruption in his early life, just by a few things he let slip.*
>
> *'When I introduced the model to him, he was very interested in it and I talked about the "there and then" in the "here and now". I talked about the healthy self and asked him when he last felt that he was in that healthy self. What was it like, how did he experience it? What was he doing, with whom and where? I used this a bit like an anchoring exercise, so he could bring a clear memory to the surface about this time.*

Then I asked something like, "what is needed for you to be able to be in that self, more often now?" I talked about resourcing himself so that he could let go some of the need to control everything so tightly.'

This coach took a slightly different approach to bring the connection with the healthy self into the foreground. The case examples above show how helpful it can be to have a fuller autobiography. You have more to work with on linking 'here and now' to 'there and then'. In this last case example, however, there is very little to work with. Focusing on the healthy self may lead to more disclosure of useful information, but there is no guarantee of course.

The world of work, the roles chosen or assigned, the relationships and the groups one becomes part of, all can re-traumatise an individual – that is, the trauma feelings from 'there and then' are activated. This results in heightened survival strategy responses. In some cases, the nature of the work itself may involve a higher risk of this re-traumatisation (for example, the armed forces, rescue services, and health and social care). When we are stuck in 'survival' we are unable to take and act on decisions which are in the best interests of our healthy self and well-being. The question *'is this healthy for me or not healthy for me?'* is a useful question to ask ourselves and have clients ask themselves. As in the example above, the coaching is about supporting the client's healthy self to find a way to a healthier work environment.

Clients who are the most challenging to work with, who reject all interventions, are the ones whose survival strategies seem to be switched to 'very high'. As a result, they may be critical, judgemental, and rejecting of your expertise, or they may appear to be unable to access the sense of self-agency needed to bring about the changes they say they desire. These are the clients that stimulate the survival strategy responses in their coaches. In response, you may switch to the direct and control mode of working, or withdraw and become passive or feel deskilled and develop a survival narrative about being a bad or ineffective coach. As a result, the coaching becomes stuck, or feels very difficult or seems not to progress very far. If you stay in your healthy self, not being judgemental but being compassionate, you will be more able to use interventions aimed at the healthy self of clients. Our first response to 'difficult clients' must be to look at how we contribute to that difficulty. Clients who are dominated by survival, however, may still not respond that well to coaching. If they want change, a therapeutic route may be the best one for them, and we can support them in accessing that option.

4   The survival self

The survival self is a complex combination of survival responses and behaviours, which I have divided into three groupings (Figure 4.1), all of which interact with one another. In this chapter, I focus on the characteristics of the survival self and why it gets in the way of coaching. I also explore the survival identity that is constructed in response to the traumatising environment of childhood.

Recognising the presence of the survival self

We meet the expression of the survival self regularly, especially when coaching is not going well. We hear it in talk that uses *must, should, always, never*. We observe it in those who want to be perfect, strong, or independent of others. It is present in particular behaviour, such as narcissism, the 'imposter syndrome', and the persona of the 'rebel'. We observe it in the use of control, rescue, criticism, and aggression. We meet it in compliant, submissive behaviour, and in those who slump into helplessness or assume a victim attitude. We meet it in ourselves when we feel deskilled or convince ourselves we are the wrong coach for the client. We often hear about it in the context of relationship problems with others and with roles and work.

We are in the presence of the survival self when there is a disregard of the impact of life choices on rest, sleep, physical and mental well-being. The survival self is not a benign self, its functioning can result in ill health, burnout, and loss of well-being.

There are some behaviours which can be healthy and which may also be a survival defence. It depends on which self it comes from – the healthy or survival self. For example, where is the boundary between motivating ourselves enough for rehabilitation after an operation, and it becoming a form of self-punishment? It is punitive when it is a means of avoiding feelings about dependency or vulnerability, where the body is seen as an enemy to be brought into line. It is healthy when we work *with* the body and there is enough rest. The survival self is not capable of authentic compassion and empathy because of its fear of intimacy with others, as this will activate the trauma feelings. As a result, when living through it we treat ourselves and others badly. It carries the internal critic, sometimes referred to in coaching as the 'gremlin'. This critic is often a response from the 'there and then'. For example, if we find we are berating ourselves for being stupid, it is probable that 'not being stupid' or being clever was expected of us as children, a condition of being loved. Any mistake we make or failure to meet the high standards we have set for ourselves is met with this self-rejection before imagined others can reject us.

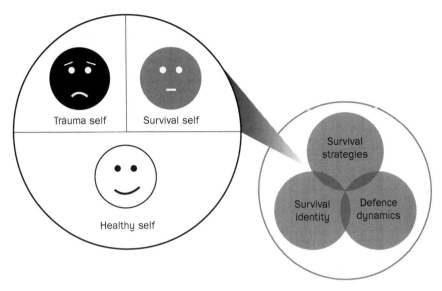

Figure 4.1 The survival self

Source: Adapted from Franz Ruppert (2012).

Characteristics of the survival self

The survival self is not coachable since it blocks the emotional experience needed for personal change. It is an ineffective or inappropriate coach. Understanding the surviving self and how it operates enables us to notice when we and our clients are operating through it, thus bringing elements into conscious awareness where they can be explored. We need to coach round the survival self, focusing on the healthy self to activate personal change. This self-awareness helps expand the healthy self and our ability to be with experience without dissociation and re-traumatisation. It is a contribution to stepping out of our trauma biography.

Our survival self develops in response to our relational environment within the context of trauma of identity, trauma of love, and trauma of sexuality. As well as suppressing the trauma feelings of fear/terror, emotional pain, rage, shame, and vulnerability, the connection with the felt body experience is also minimised. Body awareness is essential for exploring our experience. It is the background to our self-awareness. To know what emotions we feel requires this flow of information and energy between the data processing of the brain and the body. Knowing what we are feeling and are experiencing, which requires a connection with our body, is essential for healthy autonomy. This process is compromised by trauma. If a coach and client want to facilitate access to their healthy selves, they need to develop a strong flow of felt experience information to process their experience. We need to check in with ourselves regularly in sessions about what this felt experience is.

Where the flow of information is blocked by trauma, there is a disconnection with the body. The body can come to be seen as an object and not part of ourselves. As a result, we can disregard signs of physical pain or extreme tiredness, and not view them as an indication that we need to make some changes to the way we are living; instead, we often intensify the behaviour that is causing the symptoms.

Living through the survival self is exhausting, particularly for people who have been living through it for forty years or more. There is too little self-regulation, and too many stress hormones, to allow rest. It also drives out joy, vitality, our sense of freedom. These belong with the healthy self. The survival self is highly resourceful – it has had to be to survive. However, it is resourceful in keeping us locked into responses from the 'there and then'.

Since the survival self is an adaptation to the environment in the 'there and then', we can hold up a mirror to clients and invite them to explore the survival behaviour's function in the 'here and now'. We can support the contact with the felt body and the resources within the healthy self.

The survival self-dynamics should only be explored if the client is happy to do so, thus we must ask their permission first. Should we feel we 'need to get a client to tackle this survival self-behaviour' or 'help them see what they are doing', we know we are in our survival self ourselves. These are not appropriate coaching strategies and could be harmful to clients. We need to look to ourselves first and consider why the client's survival behaviour is affecting us the way it is. What does it bring up for us? We can track it back to the 'there and then' if we allow ourselves the supported reflective space to do so.

The extent to which the survival self is driving a life varies depending on our trauma biography and the self-development work done by the individual. Carrying psyche-trauma is part of the human condition – it is the extent of the fragmentation that varies from person to person. Thus, we all have a survival self. The survival self will predominate more for some than others. It will also be more predominant if the environment in the 'here and now' mimics conditions in the 'there and then'. It is a continuum with the survival self being highly predominant at one end of the scale and the healthy self being highly predominant at the other.

We might find ourselves, and our clients, at all points on this continuum at some time or another, or at a single point most of the time. The greater the trauma biography, the more complex the survival self and the least access there is to the resources of the healthy self. When this is the case, coaching is likely to be more challenging. The challenge we face is our ability to stay in contact with the healthy self. If survival is predominant in the coach or the client, therapeutic help would be valuable if change is sought.

Characteristics of the healthy self

Let's remind ourselves of the characteristics of the healthy self. Within the healthy self we can respond to and process our experience in the 'here and now', including our embodied felt experience, without activating historic pathways associated with repressing the trauma feelings. The body, mind, and emotions are working in harmony; nothing is cut off from our awareness. As a result, we know what is healthy for ourselves. This includes knowing if a relationship, role, or setting is unhealthy and acting to remove ourselves from it. We have the information flows we need to enact our own agency, so extricate ourselves from the re-traumatising context.

We have compassion and empathy, so do not attack ourselves. We know we are better at some things than others; if we make a mistake or misjudge something, we learn from it without self-recrimination. We know the difference between a project failing and being a failure ourselves. Or the difference between survival and healthy attachment, or pity masquerading as compassion, or indifference masquerading as equanimity.

We are mentally alert, able to be curious about ourselves, to reflect and learn from that reflection. We can feel joy, love, and creative energy. There is a positive engagement with life.

How the characteristics of the survival self are observed in coaching

The survival defences will be activated when people contemplate change:

> 'L came to coaching wanting to have a better work/life balance. He recognised he works more hours than is healthy for him, but despite all our work in coaching, he hasn't found any way of reducing the amount of work he does. We have looked at all kinds of possibilities and he seemed keen to try them, but then came back and said it wasn't possible.'

> 'I felt I had a bit of a breakthrough with S, she seemed really positive and motivated to change her work practices, to talk to her colleagues, and to reduce the length of her working week (she was working very long days and over the weekend, doing work at home). When she came back, nothing had changed, other than she said she had taken on another project, which she 'had' to do on top of everything else. I felt so frustrated by her.'

Such responses can occur when the behaviour change is explored superficially, without engaging the underlying fears and feelings that keep the behaviour in place. Clients may not be willing to explore these, or coaches might avoid inviting curiosity about what keeps them in place. For some clients, it can be dispiriting to be unable to bring about change:

> 'One of K's goals is to build up more creative activity time. She wants to paint and write poetry (she has written some in the past) but is finding that she is too tired and has no space. We worked on this together looking

at what might be possible, and she left motivated (I thought) to do the actions she had formulated. When she came back she felt unhappy, as she hadn't been able to do anything; in fact, she is now telling herself that she is being selfish in wanting to do that.'

K's example shows a tiredness with survival. To create the space K says she wants, she needs to be willing to look at her relationship with work and what survival attachment processes are being played out. Coaching can support that by directing enquiry to the healthy self. We need to be careful not to coach the survival self or change will get blocked.

The survival self inhibits the flow of information needed to access and process the felt experience, including 'gut feelings', and thus provides a defence against inner change. As a result, people can experience confusion or mistrust about their feelings, or not be able to describe or identify them. The most likely reason for this is that they had their emotion ignored, dismissed or relabelled in childhood. They might have been told as children, *'you mustn't feel angry'* or *'don't be so silly'*, or were given something, such as food, to shut down the distress. Some clients will be in this position:

> *'C was talking about a dilemma she was in, and felt very caught up in. I asked her what her gut instinct told her. She looked confused and said, "I don't know, I don't really feel anything." When I asked her, if she did know, what might it tell her? She said, "it tells me to leave but that is totally ridiculous. I can't possibly do that". Closing down that option. I could feel a wall coming up between us. Where there had been a moment of openness, there was nothing now.'*

It can be helpful for the client's explorations to bring the body into the client's awareness during the coaching session. For example, ask them, *'where do you feel that in your body?'* or *'what are you aware of in your body as you sit there?'*, or similar body-experience questions that will bring the body into conscious awareness. This is often not an easy sort of question for someone in survival to answer and they might refuse or dismiss the question. If a client responds with *'I don't know'* or *'I know nothing'* to a question, you can always ask, *'what does not knowing feel like?'* The invitation to enquire is aimed at the healthy self, even if the client can't access a felt sense or feeling that it is not a wasted question.

If we ask clients who are in contact with their felt body-based experience what emotions are uppermost, they are likely to be able to identify where in the body they have that feeling. For example:

> *'I asked her what emotions are uppermost. Z answered that she felt a bit irritated. When I asked her where in her body she feels that, she paused and then said she could feel it in her sternum/throat area. I asked her if*

she could stay with the feeling and see what happened. She was able to and it led on to an awareness that she found very valuable about how she felt ignored, which we could then talk about. This client is able to reflect on what she feels unlike some others who I have worked with who are unable to do that and often report feeling nothing or numb.'

You may meet resistance if you bring such questions into coaching; it may startle or confuse your client. To avoid getting this response, bring the possibility into your initial conversation with the client and make it part of the contracting discussion. This provides a framework for this aspect of the work. Introducing it without preparation and the permission of the client may impair the trust the client can have in their coach. We need to be clear with clients about the elements of the coaching process they can expect.

Our own felt experience as coaches is valuable data about our responses to clients, and also in relation to the transference of feelings from clients:

'While I was with him, I was aware of some anxiety arising so took some deep breaths. I felt it was something in me, and logged it for later reflection, but I also wondered if it was something he was feeling. I decided to disclose my feeling and asked if it connected with him. He said it did and then talked about his anxiety.'

It is an important element of self-reflection to be curious about how we feel with our clients, as it is a valuable entry point into self-awareness.

In the healthy self we can feel rage, sadness, emotional pain, and grief without needing to block them or act out against others to relieve the pain. We can also feel the emotions without taking on a victim attitude, for example by thinking *'it's my fault, I always always/never/must/should . . .'*. Healthy self-emotions are those that arise spontaneously in connection with a memory or circumstance and then are released. They are intense and short-lived, appropriate to the situation, involving the body.

Survival emotions do not clearly arise from the current situation, they seem not to have a clear ending, and often last a long time or re-occur over and over. They leave the person feeling exhausted and frustrated. They are distractions from engaging with reality and are not constructive to change. However distressing they make us, their function is to keep things the same. The following example illustrates such a client and the impact on her coach:

'B, my client, used to well up with tears and cry a lot and it was hard for her and I to identify what they were in response to. It was unclear if they were tears of frustration or sadness. When I asked her about them, she told me, "they feel as if they come from an endless pool and I feel worse not better from the crying. There feels no end to them. I'm not really sure

what they are about. Sometimes they just pour out. I try very hard not to cry at work but often I have to go into the ladies as I can feel the tears coming. I just feel pathetic." We did some work with that self-attack but I was at a bit of a loss about the crying. Asking her about it seemed to bring her back from them but I knew they would come back when we looked at future possibilities.'

This client is in survival, hence the coach's confusion. It is common for there to be no felt connection in the presence of a person expressing a survival emotion, as in the following example:

> 'N cries a lot, without any resolution. When she cries I realise I don't feel anything really other than maybe some boredom. With other clients who cry when talking about an experience or memory, I feel touched by their emotion. With N, there is nothing.'

With any expression of emotion by clients, we need to be careful of our own survival responses, which may be to rush to reassure or to rescue them from what they are feeling. We may subtly make it clear that we find their emotional outburst uncomfortable. Sometimes when in the survival emotion, the individual may have an unconscious desire to be rescued or looked after, but this is a 'there and then' response that we need to avoid becoming caught up in.

Survival anger can be used to push people away, and its volume is usually in direct proportion to the amount of trauma feelings being stimulated and which must be repressed. Angry clients can be difficult and challenging:

> 'Y, the client, is so angry all the time. It is why he was referred to coaching. I find it so hard to be with him. He gets angry with me too. I am able though to stay calm and tell him it is not okay to shout at me and that if he continues, I will end the session. I said I could see how angry he was and invited him to think about the impact of his anger on others and did say something about the impact on me. This seemed to calm him a bit and I was then able to invite him to explore where the anger came from and what it was about. He was able to do that.'

If this coach was triggered by the anger, because of his own 'there and then' experience, he might have moved straight to survival. Through that he might have shouted back, or stormed out, or collapsed under the attack. No coach needs to stay in the room with an angry client who is unable to control him or herself. However, it is how we handle it that is important. It will have a different impact if from our healthy self than if from our survival self.

Expressions of feelings from the survival self do not bring healing or relief. This is not to imply that when expressed they shouldn't be met with empathy and compassion, as signs of underlying trauma. However, although hard for clients to experience, they are not harbingers of change. Survival emotions can be confusing for coaches, and distressing and shaming for clients. The options we have are to offer enquiry or feedback, for example:

> *'I see how deeply distressed you are. What can you tell me about these feelings?'*

> *'I have noticed that it seems difficult to talk about what you want (or future possibilities or what the trigger is for the client) without these tears and distress. What do you make of that?'*

> *'I see part of you is very distressed, what can you tell me about this part?'* (by using the term 'part' we are opening up room for the healthy self to talk if it is able to).

> *'What might this part of you be protecting or needing?'*

The survival identity

One of the elements of the survival self is survival identity. This is a set of characteristics and behaviour pattern that become ways in which we think about and describe ourselves.

The survival 'I' (identity) evolves in response to our early relationships. It develops in place of the healthy sense of ourselves, which is not welcomed or encouraged by those around us. We learn to take on characteristics to survive our environment as children. This sense of our identity comes to be experienced as

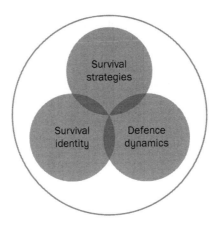

Figure 4.2 Components of the survival self

the 'apparently normal self' (Ogden and Fisher, 2015) but is made up of survival responses.

To develop a healthy connection with, and sense of, ourselves and to develop our innate talents and abilities, we need to be nurtured in a way that welcomes this. Parents need to respond sensitively and calmly, being willing to put their own needs to one side. We need to be wanted for ourselves rather than as objects that might gratify the needs of our parents.

Secure attachment patterns facilitate this connection with a healthy sense of ourselves. The split psyche model illustrates that we all have a healthy self that continues to be available to us, and carries resources of self-reflection, self-compassion, awareness, and emotional contact with ourselves. However, its strength and our capacity to access the resources within it are directly related to the depth of our trauma biography.

Before language, we start to build up an 'idea' of ourselves through how those close to us respond. We see and feel the carer's responses to us, how they hold us, how they talk to us and what tone they use, how they respond to our needs. After language, we take in who we are told we are, the narratives given to us and those we create, and the identifications we make. All of these are open to exploration if the healthy self is strong enough to reflect and enquire into this assumed identity and the feelings that lie deep behind it.

We listen for these elements of the survival identity when talking about ourselves or exploring the biography of and in our exchanges with a client. We hear what the client has taken in and 'believes' about him or herself. A statement like '*I am the sort of person who . . .*', is always a statement about survival. The survival 'I' is shaped in response to trauma of identity, trauma of love, and trauma of sexuality when the child is seen as an object and objectified. As I have set out, there are a range of reasons this may occur, from conception onwards, all in response to traumatised parents. From the start, the baby may have been conceived to fulfil the needs of the mother or partnership, or despite the wishes of the mother or partner, or to replace a child who died, or to fulfil parental expectations and aspirations.

I have talked before about how narratives are given to children in ways that leave out the pain and distress to the child or emphasise the distress to the person sharing the story rather than the impact on the child. Families keep secrets, even though some in the family have a sense that something is being kept hidden. Families create illusions, and the truth is not always told. When, as adults, we want to ask questions, it may be that our parents are infirm or have died, making it difficult to get answers or to seek clarification.

Children are often attributed characteristics by their parents that don't really apply, yet end up defining them. The following are some examples:

'*You are the bright one of the family.*'

'*You will always need to work hard.*'

'*You are too big or small to do X.*'

'*You are the pretty one.*'

'*Your brother will always be brighter than you.*'

'*You are over-sensitive.*'

'*You are frail or strong.*'

A parent need not speak directly to the child but instead imply some attribute through their behaviour towards the child. I remember desperately wanting a pair of ballet shoes aged nine but being told I was too tall for ballet. That stuck with me. Whether I was actually told I was too tall, or it is something that was somehow relayed to me, I don't know, but it is a message I carry. The reason may have been so as not to pay for ballet lessons, or because attending lessons would have been too difficult to arrange. In the end it doesn't really matter why; what matters now is why I hold on to it and the impact it continues to have. Children take these attributions as givens, and continue to believe them unquestioningly as adults. Coaching can help this exploration and facilitate challenge where clients are willing.

Identifications are aspects of other people we absorb to fill the gap left by being unable to grow our healthy sense of ourselves. For example, at an unconscious level, children may decide '*I want to be like my father*' or '*I want to be the total opposite of my father*'. Both are ways of claiming an identity. We also take in, and make ours, the survival strategies of our parents. We unconsciously model ourselves on them. We can also identify with our clients and focus on supporting their change rather than looking to addressing our own needs for change.

Gender conditioning also brings identification possibilities. We are told what little girls or boys should be like, given toys and clothing, pink for a girl and blue for a boy, to reinforce those characteristics, and be taught what our position in life is. We may absorb the expectations and limitations as 'givens' or we may become rebels against them; both are survival identities.

Identifications with roles, diagnoses, feelings, and behaviours are survival strategies that continue throughout life. We may decide that belonging to a particular profession or identifying with a particular belief system or sports team is a central part of who we are and consider no other option. It has the same driven quality of all survival behaviour. We may hear indications of this in what clients say about their chosen profession:

> '*I am a lawyer through and through, although I find the work very stressful and I'd love to do something else, but I couldn't contemplate not being a barrister.*'

This client clearly appears to identify with a profession through her survival self. There is no room to explore alternatives. Where identity is from identification, the tendency is to cling to or be dependent on that identification. Rather than changing career, people will stay in a job or with a company for far longer than is good for their career or well-being. For example:

> 'When I look back, I realise I should have left X far sooner than I did. I don't know why I didn't really. I felt it was part of who I was to do that work. I should have left about three years before I eventually did. When it came to leave, it felt really hard, as if I was losing part of myself.'

These are also examples of insecure attachment, clinging on despite the environment being non-nurturing. This is a pattern from the 'there and then' with perhaps the belief that '*if I stay I will eventually get the love and recognition I need*' and '*if I leave I will be all alone*'.

Some people never find a lasting survival identification and move from one profession or role to another, or from one spiritual practice to another in the search for one.

> 'Ken had had a very varied career. He started off as a social worker, then decided to retrain as a teacher, and taught for a few years. He then saw an opportunity to change direction and become a trainer in businesses, doing a further qualification in the process. He kept waiting for a feeling of meaning and fulfilment but that didn't come. He also noticed he was getting very tired and couldn't seem to shake it off. He then considered retraining again to become a coach, which he did. In supervision, he talked about how he still didn't feel he had found the best match for him but couldn't do anything now as he had financial responsibilities.'

Throughout his career, Ken had been effective and successful. He pushed himself to do well, but never felt satisfied with his work and life. Ken was being driven by his survival self, looking for an identity that would bring meaning for him. Unconsciously, he was possibly looking for a sense of belonging, being loved and wanted, that was missing from the 'there and then'. In the process, he became exhausted and felt a loss of vitality and spark.

We also use identifications with emotions as determinants of identity. This occurs when we say, '*I'm angry*' or '*I'm depressed*'. Listen how different it sounds to say, '*Part of me feels angry*' or '*Part of me feels depressed*'. Here, the 'I' is separated from the emotion, and by so doing, we are giving space for the healthy self's 'I' to enquire about that identification. If you hear clients identifying with a feeling, encourage them to reframe the statement from '*I am ...*' to '*Part of me feels ...*'. From that point you can enquire, if the client is willing, about the quality of the feeling and where it comes from.

The same can occur with diagnoses. People may say, '*I am diabetic*' or '*he is bipolar*'. We can release the survival identification by saying, '*I have diabetes*' or *'he is diagnosed with bipolar disorder'*. We need to be careful with our language or we, too, will be making attributions.

Trauma of sexuality is also expressed via the survival self through the poor recognition or protection of personal boundaries or in how sexuality is expressed or used. Although the latter can be a major issue for some people, sex and sexuality rarely raised in coaching, as it is something that is not easily talked about by clients and might be avoided by coaches.

Parenting styles from the survival self

Parenting styles that come from the survival self produce survival self-adaptations in children. The extent to which the survival self of the parent is doing the parenting will of course depend on the trauma biography of the parent. The list of style possibilities is extensive, but includes over-protection, bullying, under-protection, pseudo-affection, idealisation (for example, the child can do no wrong), setting rigid regimes and expectations, setting no regimes or boundaries, and confused styles moving from one approach to another. Such parenting can result in the child feeling unsafe, unloved, and unwanted.

Our place in the birth order has an impact in terms of the time and attention that can be given to young infants. Also, a sibling with a disability, a chronic illness, or who has died will have an impact on the time and attention that caregivers can devote to the other children. Companionship is possible among siblings. Sometimes they can support each other within a difficult environment and bonds are formed. Sometimes they can be part of the traumatising environment in the case of bullying and sexual abuse. Parents respond to their children differently: some compare one child with another, or subtly make it appear that one sibling's needs are more important. This can become part of the survival self's narrative and attributions. Children in the same family do not experience the same upbringing. Each child's genetic inheritance, family order, and experience are unique, as is their response to the environment.

We also create our own stories to help us understand our experience. If our experience as a child was that we didn't feel loved or liked, we might then assume that *'we are not lovable or likable because, if we were, why wouldn't our mother or father have loved us?'* Children take responsibility for their experience, as it is too distressing to think that our parents were unable to want, love, and/or protect us. We carry these self-beliefs deep in our survival self.

From these painful experiences we may create an unconscious narrative with which we then identify and which becomes part of our survival identity. For example:

> *'If I work or try hard, then I will be loved or recognised.'*

> *'If I keep my head down, no one will criticise me.'*

'If I don't shout loudly, no one will attend to me.'

'I must look after others, then maybe they will look after me or not leave me.'

'Being perfect will keep me safe.'

'I have to constantly prove myself, as deep down I know I am not really good enough.'

'I don't rely on anyone really, as I know people always let me down.'

These are expressions of trauma of love. If the survival behaviour is open to exploration, some clients will be able to articulate what is caught up in the behaviour.

We also create narratives from the attributions and identifications about our talents, the limits to those talents, and what we believe we can do or not do. The coaching challenges of *'Who told you that?'* and *'Where does that thought come from?'* are useful interventions. Likewise, where there appears to be an identification or entanglement with a role or profession, we can enquire:

> *'What do you fear might happen if you were to change direction?'* and/or *'What might you gain by changing direction?'*
>
> *'In what ways might you have been drawn to this career path by other people's expectations and attributes to you?'* or *'In what ways might you be identifying with someone in your family by taking on this role?'*

'What do you want?' is a useful question to ask several times to help get a deeper answer from the healthy self. In the survival self, the *wants* sound more like *'I would like to'*, *'I hope I may be able to'*, and *'I think I have to'*. The answer from the healthy self is *'I want . . .'* with no hesitation.

Some people respond to parenting styles by becoming compliant, while others may become rebellious. This is typically part of adolescent development and usually passes. However, in some it becomes a core part of the survival self. People who adopt the role of rebel feel they must avoid conforming and often do so in a hostile or aggressive way. The adult healthy self can challenge the imposition of norms but will either leave a place that doesn't require adaptation beyond that deemed acceptable, or challenge in a direct non-violent way. The client example that follows illustrates how rebelling might present in coaching:

> *'Jane prided herself on being the rebel. She was the first to challenge management and anyone who made any assumptions. She saw this as her "life's work" in some ways. She made enemies and failed to carry people with her, so was often left isolated. However, when she was in full flight,*

she of course got everyone's attention and time. She felt victimised but had no solutions for what she wanted, instead she said: "that's up to them, they're senior management". She came into coaching after a performance review; her new boss saw real talent in her but felt her behaviour was going to sabotage any success she might be capable of. Her early story was a sad one of being moved from family to family. As trust built between us, she was willing to explore this rebel identity, and the purpose it served. We looked at which parts of it she liked and which parts she could see were harming her. We then looked at what would be healthier for her.'

The coach here was careful to encourage the client to explore this role of rebel she had adopted. It took time to establish enough safety for Jane to want to explore this identification. She had to be willing and give permission. She was then able to consider where it might have come from and what function it served in the 'there and then' and now served in the 'here and now'. The coach also asked about what aspects Jane wanted to keep. For example, standing up against injustice can be done from the healthy self. This is a process of disentangling the survival identification through the client's self-exploration. Coaches need to be sure they are not in a survival attachment themselves with the referring organisation, as they might handle this client very differently, for example by wanting to turn her into a more compliant employee or by being in denial about any adverse work conditions.

Addressing the question of 'who we are in our own right' is one that could take us in all kinds of different directions philosophically. Within the context of psyche-trauma, it refers to the healthy self, without the influence of stress- and trauma-induced neuropathways associated with fight, flight, or freeze. That healthy self is connected to our felt experience, in the here and now, and can reflect on what is healthy for us and make decisions that promote our well-being without fear of recrimination or rejection. Dominance by a survival identity is damaging to our well-being and vitality. To change how we respond to the environment, we need to explore these givens and be prepared to let them go.

Survival relationships with work

Jane's behaviour above was an example of a survival relationship with work. Our relationship with work is affected by the dynamics within our survival self.

A healthy work environment is one where there are challenges in which we feel sufficiently stimulated, and which provide for our social needs. There is no anxiety or stress outside that which can be easily regulated. We are within our zone of competence and talent, and able to push at the edges of that zone. We are also able to tolerate being taken outside our comfort zone, when and if that happens.

A survival approach to roles or work brings exhaustion, lack of enjoyment, and a range of survival behaviours. A work addition, the compulsion to work long hours, has its roots in an unconscious survival belief that doing so will keep us safe, or loved, or wanted, or not abandoned. Who we are at work, and who we believe we need to be to survive, can be at odds with who we are at home. The survival self might be uppermost at work, or at home, or in both, but show itself in different ways. This is relevant to all work–life balance conversations.

Someone who has a strong survival need to be perfect also tends to be indecisive, avoids completing tasks, and exaggerates any error or misjudgement. Criticism from outside is very painful and there will be an active internal critic. Such individuals believe that working hard should itself result in success, as the following example illustrates.

> '*I have worked and tried hard all my working life, it's just how I am. I drive myself hard and I want my team to achieve a lot too. I was shocked when my boss, out of the blue, told me that some of my team had said I harass and bully them. I do push people but I don't bully them. My boss also said that he has asked me often about getting projects in on time and that he isn't getting what he needs from me in terms of outcomes. I felt devastated and angry to be honest as I work so hard, I work late into the evening, and am constantly revising papers to get them right. I have missed a few deadlines recently, but the end product was so much better, even though I could have done more with more time. I can't believe he said those things to me as I just work so hard for him and the company. I can't understand why he is picking on me.*'

This client is locked into a survival enactment in work. The first step is to ask if she is interested in exploring how she is at work, as it seems that it is not going well for her right now. If she isn't willing to, you are likely to work only at a cognitive level, which might bring small behaviour change but will not bring the survival self behaviour into conscious awareness where it can be worked with. However, if she is willing, you could use the 'split in the psyche model' and enquire into the possible 'there and then' connections. You can enquire about what the function of working or trying so hard might be for her. It sounds like established survival behaviour, so small steps are likely. However, each step is a step closer to her healthy self.

Other people survive by not working hard, or not being able to find their place in the world of work. They may try one thing, then another, but always feel a deep dissatisfaction and lack of passion, or ambition. They may find it hard to get in contact with their healthy self, to find out what they really want for themselves and their life. It could be that they carried high expectations from their family, which they do not want to fulfil but are afraid of taking assertive action. It could be that little was expected of them or that they got little reward or recognition. We can explore hypotheses with the client if it seems appropriate, linking with the 'there and then'. Career coaching may not be successful with individuals embedded in this survival expression, as they may be unable to explore the function of their dissatisfaction with work. As with all clients, it is essential that they have personally contracted for coaching – and not had it imposed on them – and have set their own intentions or wanted outcomes for the work.

Here is a client who didn't find his own coach, but came to please his sister, and who has problems with finding meaningful work:

> 'John was referred to coaching by his sister, who felt he needed some help to get a grip of his career, whatever that might turn out to be. He wasn't sure it would help but came to please his sister. When I asked him about him and work, he said he felt all he had done was a waste of time and that he just felt he had ended up in a cul-de-sac with no way out. He wanted to be in the theatre but he didn't, he wanted to write but didn't, he said he knew he was supposed to connect with his passion but he felt nothing. I found it hard to get any sense of him about what he wanted to use the coaching for. I talked about what I could offer, and what therapy might offer, and suggested that he go away and think about what would be helpful for him to address the situation he is in.'

If this client returns, it might be helpful for the coach to explore using interventions to engage passion, feelings, and joy, without any connection with work, as a way into activating the healthy self. You can reflect what you observe in his behaviour and enquire if he is interested in exploring this relationship with work. If so, you can offer ways to think about it. It is possible the idea of doing what he wants is so terrifying, that it is to be avoided at all cost.

Sometimes the energy of the survival self collapses, leaving depression and apathy and a withdrawal from work through absence. The body can also 'collapse' if it has been subjected to stress for a long time; it makes it impossible to continue to work. Withdrawal from work can result in social isolation, which is painful. This is unlikely to be resolved by coaching; although as before, if a client contracts for coaching, you can support them in accessing the resources they need to address the underlying issues. The client in the following example had withdrawn from work:

> 'I was asked to see Mary, with her permission, even though she was on sick leave with stress, by her boss. I checked out with him what his motivation was for that, and why weren't HR working with her. He said he valued her as a member of staff and wanted her back. She came in to see me. She had had a number of periods off sick and reported feeling very stressed every time she thought of work and was being treated for depression. When I asked her what her goals might be for this coaching,

she said she didn't have any. She said it wasn't the job so much, she just didn't feel able to work. I explored with her what other social support networks she had – they were very few. She is being treated by the GP but feels on her own with it all. I reflected that I wondered if counselling or therapy might be helpful, as I wasn't sure coaching was going to be useful at this time, maybe later when she was feeling less depressed. I left it there with her. Did I do the right thing?'

My response is 'yes', the coach did the right thing. If there is no contract with the client, the coach may want to be seen to be a helpful coach, rescuing the client ignoring the likelihood of coaching not working.

Burnout is a collapse of the survival strategies and behaviours which enable withdrawal. Burnout is usually the result of illusions about working hard to please others, to get love and recognition. As such, it is an expression of trauma of love. It could be a case of the healthy self saying, *'enough is enough, no more'* and forcing an opportunity for reflection and revision. It depends how clients respond to this call from the body and 'spirit': whether they take it as an opportunity to do some deeper work and let go of the survival structures, or to stay stuck in the survival withdrawal. If you are working with someone nearing burnout, it helps to be aware that this is a survival response.

For any client who is exhausted and tired owing to their survival self-behaviour, you can ask them:

> *'Is it possible that you are using this approach to your work in order not to feel difficult emotions?'*
>
> *'By dumbing down those emotions, might you also have blocked out the emotions of joy and excitement?'*

While these are closed questions, to which the answer can be 'yes' or 'no', they are openings to further possible enquiry. We are raising an idea.

Other predominant survival self-expressions we meet in the workplace are those of narcissism, and what is called 'imposter syndrome', which I talk about in Chapter 6.

Coaching around the survival self

As always, the important starting point is with yourself before you start rushing to diagnose or identify survival strategies in others. Recall work with a client that felt as if it didn't go well; focus on your responses, motivations, and feelings. Which of the following apply?

You sacrificed something important to you to make room for the client's schedule.	You recognised you rushed through the contracting process and missed some important things out.
Instead of offering the client feedback in the here and now, you took refuge in avoidance and politeness, while feeling frustrated.	You felt exasperated and tried everything with this client.
You were bored, watching the clock, not engaging with the client.	You felt irritated and that the client's issues were trivial.
You felt deep pity and went out of your way to be very helpful or reassuring.	You realise you spoke very sharply to the client several times, and were rather pushy.
You felt you did all the work, and found each session exhausting.	You noticed you were talking a lot.
You thought you weren't the right person to coach X, that you lacked the necessary skills, even though you feel competent with others.	You found yourself talking negatively about the client to a colleague and you wanted to end the programme of coaching.

Each session that seems not to go well, or you find the client less responsive to coaching – or you – than others, offers us a wonderful opportunity for deep self-reflection. You can reflect on your responses and track them back, asking for example:

'What was really going on for me?'

'What was I feeling?'

'What had happened to my connection with my body?'

'Who might the client have become for me?'

'What associations with my "there and then" emerge as I reflect on this encounter?'

'What was I feeling with the client?'

'What was I afraid of?'

'What might be behind that?'

The more we use this reflective enquiry by ourselves and in supervision, the more we will learn about the internalised trauma dynamics and the more able we will be to recognise and connect with those in the client.

Your own approach to your work may also give you an opportunity to reflect on *'how might my survival self be operating here and for what reason?'* How about your own self-beliefs, narratives, and attributes? The more we are able to recognise the elements of our own adaptive identity and survival behaviour, and their triggers, the more available our healthy self will become for attending to the client.

Coaching around the survival self in the client

- We need to use attuned listening, to be in good contact with clients and to listen for survival vocabulary. When we hear it, we can reflect it back to clients with an enquiry about 'there and then'.
- We need to use interventions aimed at involving the healthy self in enquiry.
- We can explore the links between the 'there and then' and the 'here and now'. We can use the 'split to the psyche' model as education.
- We can use coaching exercises that work with self-limiting beliefs. These beliefs are usually the legacy of attributes and narrative.
- We can give our observations when clients' behaviour is damaging for them.
- We can help clients develop their contact with the felt-experience in the body, helping them access affect and name emotions accurately for themselves.
- We can ask the types of coaching questions given in this chapter and in the box above, adapting them for clients.
- We can challenge narratives and identifications, inviting enquiries about where they came from. We can support the client to bring survival behaviour into consciousness so that it can be explored.

To step out of our trauma biography, we need to dig deep into our awareness with the aid of a therapeutic process. However, coaching clients can explore the characteristics and stories of the survival self and decide what to let go of. It is important that a replacement narrative isn't another survival narrative but is as near the truth as is possible to achieve. We can only make these interventions with clients' permission and if they have enough healthy self to engage with that level of self-enquiry and self-awareness. If clients are non-responsive to such enquiries, first look to yourself and if your survival self is getting in the way. Then, reflect on the nature of the contract and the client's stated intentions or goals for the work. What are they coming for? Who are they coming for? Look at any survival behaviour you have brought into the contracting.

The next step is to observe how much of the client's healthy self seems to be available to you when you meet and between sessions:

- How much capacity is there for personal reflection and enquiry?
- How much access is there to the felt inner and body experience?

- How much does the client seem to identify with the work/social role they have taken on?
- To what extent does the client engage in intellectualisation, or logical rationale? What feelings are they able to express?
- If I give feedback about what I observe, is the client interested, or do they dismiss it?
- How do I feel with the client, do I feel pushed away or pulled towards, or held at a distance?
- How much joy and enthusiasm does the client express about their work and life?

If the capacity for accessing the healthy self is compromised by the survival self's predominance, what coaching is able to contribute will be more limited. It also makes coaches more vulnerable to coaching through their survival self to avoid feelings of helplessness, failure, criticism by others, loss of status, being rejected, unseen, and/or not valued.

5 Defence dynamics of the survival self

In this chapter, I focus on the defence dynamics element of the survival self as identified by Ruppert (2012, 2014), which involves the perpetrator–victim dynamic and entangled, or co-dependent, relationships. Like all elements of the survival self, they are interconnected and regularly met in coaching. Through recognising them, we can raise self-awareness, enquire into their roots, and use resources in the healthy self to respond differently to the environment.

Perpetrator and victim defence dynamics

Psyche-trauma results from the interaction between a victim, the person who is affected – emotionally, psychologically, physiologically, physically – and one or more perpetrators, the environment of the uterus or those on whom we are dependent. People who parent through their survival self are perpetrators in the sense of the impact they have on the child's developing psyche. Those who use physical or sexual violence are also perpetrators. Using the term 'perpetrator' may alarm you. However, I encourage you to step aside from such a response in order to explore how the perpetrator–victim dynamic is internalised and acted out within the survival self.

Traumatised adults carry with them the internalised feeling memory of being a victim in childhood. That is, they have feelings of rage, helplessness, vulnerability, and shame. Remember that the stress hormones of fight or flight are not able to protect the child; instead, the freeze response occurs, bringing dissociation and fragmentation. We carry that victim experience in our psyche.

Becoming a perpetrator on others or on ourselves, through self-harm, is a survival strategy deployed to keep the trauma feelings suppressed. Being a perpetrator ourselves is a survival identification with the original perpetrator and their power over us in the 'there and then'. In self-perpetration, we are continuing the work of the original perpetrator by harming ourselves through self-attack, physical harm, addictions, and issues with food. In perpetration on others, we are passing on that damage and pain. This acting out, particularly through violence and anger, is re-traumatising for the individual doing the harm. In physical abuse, the abuser is out of control, distracting themselves from their own pain or inner chaos. They gain some release through their perpetration and may or may not feel remorse. Either way, the act of harming others brings a further split in the psyche, adding to the trauma biography. People who are serial perpetrators, therefore, have suffered

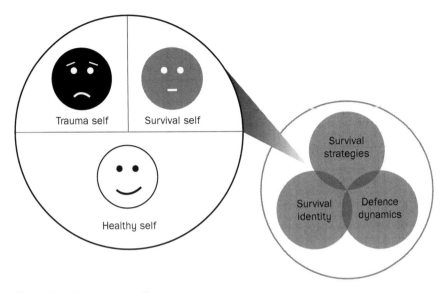

Figure 5.1 The survival self

Source: Adapted from Franz Ruppert (2012).

many splits to the psyche and move further and further away from being able to access a healthy self.

Dr Christine Dickson, a domestic abuse therapist in the USA, has created a very helpful diagram to show the cycle of abuse (http://www.trivalleypsychotherapy.com/trauma-abuse.html). This cycle consists of three phases, the first being the abuse itself, which is followed by a faux-reconciliation or remorse phase, of making amends, and attempts at forgiving or forgetting that the abuse ever occurred. In a work setting, this second phase of faux-reconciliation might involve the perpetrator saying how much they respect or value their victim and how they are irreplaceable. However, the damage is done. The victim feels frightened and does all they can to soothe the perpetrator and to avoid provocation, even though they have no idea what such provocation might be. This phase cannot be sustained and moves into the third phase where the relationship begins to break down again, tensions rise, resulting in further abuse. And so the cycle continues. At the core of the cycle is denial, by both parties in this co-dependent relationship. Where this is an experience from childhood, the experience results in a heightened release of stress hormones and a hypervigilance that is active throughout life and ready to be triggered by anything in the 'here and now' that mimics that earlier experience.

An example might be of clients who work with managers who are highly critical, demanding, and undermining, and then say '*sorry, I was under so much pressure, I didn't mean it, I really value your work*', but who then repeat the bullying behaviour once the relationship tensions have built up again. This is difficult for most people. However, those who have experienced perpetration in the 'there and then' are more likely to become a submissive victim of this manager, trying hard to please them and avoid triggering the bullying once again. They are likely to become highly stressed and their performance will dip, making them even more of a target for the bully.

In the 'here and now' of coaching, we are unlikely to hear about violence. Domestic abuse is rarely talked about because it is often deeply shaming, and most workplaces do not tolerate violent abuse. As coaches we will hear about non-violent perpetration and its impact on clients and those they work with. We might also experience it ourselves from coaching sponsors, clients or colleagues.

Consider the following questions about potential examples of perpetration:

- Is a bully perpetrating on others?
- Is someone hitting another person perpetrating on them?
- Is someone who uses high levels of control over themselves and others perpetrating on themselves and the others?
- Is sexual harassment, sexual assault, and/or rape perpetration?
- Is self-harming in all its forms – including working until exhausted, hurting oneself physically, limiting food intake to minimal levels – self-perpetration?
- Is stealing from someone a perpetration, including all the subtle ways of stealing, such as stealing ideas or credit for work?
- What about rescuing others whom we see as needing help or protection? Is it perpetration under the guise of kindness or helpfulness? (Unless it is about a life-saving intervention or protection from harm, when it is an immediate response to a circumstance.)

Yes, all of the above are examples of perpetration. Although it might be obvious to you that sexual assault, for example, is a form of perpetration, the perpetrator might not see it that way.

Victim survival attitudes

Both victims and perpetrators develop survival attitudes (Ruppert, 2014) to overcome the traumatising experience. These become part of the survival self and are expressed to deny and suppress the trauma feelings associated with the traumatising experience. The cut-off feelings are not silent, however, but are regularly stimulated by events in the 'here and now', producing the victim survival attitudes – which include perpetration – and perpetrator survival attitudes.

The survival attitudes of victims are well documented from the work done with victims of sexual abuse. They are not confined to victims of such abuse, however, but all victims of perpetration. If you hear such attitudes in the coaching room, you may be able to challenge them and show they are typical responses of victims, thereby normalising them.

The following example is of a client who is showing one of the victim survival responses, that of defence:

> '*Claire came to coaching through a recommendation from her boss during a performance review in which Claire's performance was not meeting the boss's requirements. Claire was very upset but decided to take up the coaching offer. Claire had been in her role for twelve months, she said it was very pressurised, that people were dismissive and competitive. She found her boss critical and hard to please. How she described his behaviour and the impact on her sounded to me as if she was being consistently bullied. She defended his behaviour saying, "I expect it is me, I am not an easy person to get to know; he is just under so much pressure himself; I am just frustrated with myself for not getting things right; no, it's not bullying".*'

The following is another survival response, this time that of denial:

> '*Well, yes I was sexually abused by my uncle when I was eight or nine, but I think I was looking for some attention, and I refuse to think I am a victim; it's all in the past now and nothing to do with the present.*'

The victim survival attitudes shown by these two examples involve defending or protecting the perpetrator, taking the blame or denying the impact.

'*They didn't mean it*'; '*They couldn't help it.*'	This is a way of protecting the perpetrator and of denying one's own story being told or honouring one's own experience.
'*It was my fault, I asked for it, I should have/ shouldn't have . . .*'	This is the response of many victims and is particularly crippling for victims of sexual abuse, who typically blame themselves. It protects the perpetrator.
'*I am so angry with myself for letting it happen.*'	Many victims blame themselves. Part of the trauma response is dissociation and freezing. Our ability to act is diminished.
'*It didn't happen.*'	Straightforward denial.
'*I hate being called a victim; I refuse to think like that.*'	Denying the impact and protecting the perpetrator. No one wants to feel a victim, with the associated feelings of shame, vulnerability, and helplessness. However, it is possible to acknowledge being a victim of perpetration without identifying with the term 'victim' as part of one's survival identity. It doesn't need to define who we are.

If there is a childhood history of abuse and love being confused, as with sexual abuse within a family or close community, as adults those victims may not be able to recognise perpetrators. Having had their boundaries ignored as children, they are less able to protect their personal boundaries and themselves. This leaves them constantly vulnerable to establishing co-dependent relationships. They might unconsciously welcome perpetrators into their life, whether at work or outside work, and set up a repeated pattern, as in the following example:

> '*Jennifer told a story of repeated problems at work, over a number of job changes. It always started off really well, she liked her boss or team mate a lot, and was sure it would all work well. Then things turned sour and they bullied or sexually harassed her. She was sure it was her fault, something she was doing, as they had all seemed so nice.*'

Here is a client who cannot recognise perpetrators until they harm her. Even then, she protects them and blames herself. It is possible that this pattern rules her personal life as well. She may be helped to see connections between the 'here and now' and the 'there and then' if there are accounts of her being abused as a child. Often those are left out of biographies in coaching. However, you can offer your observation that she appears not to recognise people who will harm her. It is important to be careful when inviting self-reflection not to imply that it is the fault of the client that apparently 'nice' people turn into perpetrators. The client must be in her healthy self to address this. The important focus is what is healthy for her now and what might help her protect herself in the future?

The confusion of love with abuse, arising from the trauma of love and trauma of sexuality, may also mean that a person, while recognising the signs of a perpetrator in another, moves towards that other person with the aim of neutralising the situation in the hope of preventing an attack:

> '*I find him very difficult to work with, critical and off-putting, but I thought it was really important we collaborate on our shared project. I decided to get closer to him, hoping that that would make him friendlier and less hostile. I do things I think will be helpful and volunteer to do tasks for the project, hoping that will ease things between us. However, it feels as if he is always "biting" me, I feel pushed away and hurt. How can I change my approach?*'

This is a client who uses his survival resources of denial and survival attachment to get closer in the hope of reconciliation, only to be repeatedly hurt. When exploring his history, this made sense to him as a pattern from 'there and then'. He was able to see this as a learned survival behaviour and explored how to move into a healthier place from which to relate to his colleague. If there are no given links in the biography, you can offer your observation of what you see happening and ask if that feels right.

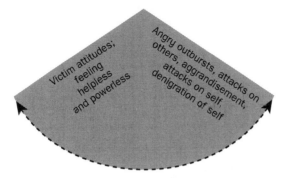

Figure 5.2 Victim survival attitudes

Another aspect of victim survival attitudes is the internalisation within the survival self of both victimhood and aggression. The sense of victimhood, of being helpless and under the power of others, is a response to avoid acting in the 'here and now'. It is stimulated by feelings from the 'there and then'. We feel helpless, maybe hopeless, and dispirited. We can become overwhelmed by these feelings. We may complain about things and people. However, when explored we can recognise that, as adults, we can act in favour of our well-being and shift our inner narrative.

We swing from one set of attitudes to the other (Figure 5.2), which can result in sudden outbursts of anger or the decision to take out our anger on innocent others – other people in the 'here and now' who come to be seen as perpetrators. We can become self-aggrandising, with a sense of superiority over others, or the aggression becomes self-reflexive, self-castigating, and self-denigrating.

Rescuing

If a person says *'Being a rescuer is just how I am'*, this is a survival identification or attribution. Most rescuers feel resentment towards those they rescue, in that they resent the time, effort, and loss of pleasure the rescuing involved. Some years ago, I faced the hard realisation that for a long time I had used 'kindness' as a masquerade for rescuing – I don't think this is unique. Each time I tried to rescue someone, I came to realise I ended up feeling frustrated, irritated, insufficiently thanked, and hurt. I could feel the difference between this masquerade and when I was compassionate and empathetic from my healthy self.

Rescuing is a form of perpetration that is part of the victim survival response. It is self-perpetration, in that it results in our putting our well-being and healthy needs to one side, in service to the perceived or projected needs for help of another. It is not a negotiated process with the other person, so often it is also a subtle taking control over the life of the other. We decide our help is what the person needs and jump in. The following client was distracting herself from her feelings of vulnerability by rescuing her boss:

> '*Diana was a highly experienced senior manager. In exploring her goal of reducing her work hours and commitments, we mapped out her work and how it fitted her role responsibilities over the previous two weeks. It became apparent that many hours had been spent "supporting" her colleague, going to meetings for her, getting papers finished for her, going to meetings with her when she didn't really need to, and networking with people on her behalf. When I observed that this looked like rescuing, she defended it in terms of the importance of the work.*'

While this is a case of rescuing, it also enables Diana to have a lot more control over the work. A coach working with Diana might encourage her to explore what is happening at a feelings level and explore links with the 'there and then' about feelings of lack of safety and fear of failure. This exploration may support behaviour change that allows a softening of the rescue strategy. It is likely that this way of relating is well established as a survival process.

In the following example, the client has taken her rescuing survival strategy into her relationship with the work itself, as her coach describes:

> '*Rebecca had a senior responsibility within social services. She identified with the clients and wanted to save them all. She had recognised the impact of this on her sleep and workload, and that she was getting angry with people and being side-lined. She wanted to explore changing her job. The alternative roles and organisations she contemplated all had the same dynamic of wanting to rescue people from their experience. I pointed this out to her, and she was shocked to recognise that was what she was doing. We then went on to explore how this might relate to the "there and then" and what would be healthy for her in the "here and now".*'

This client's survival identifications and need to rescue had fed her success for some time. However, it had begun to take its toll on her health and well-being, and it wasn't sustainable. Rescuing here was about trying to save others, as the pain of their suffering was too great since she identified with it. The connections are likely to be there with her early experience and perhaps some feelings about her survival.

Coaches and therapists, and I think women more than men, are vulnerable to rescuing clients. The unconscious trade is, '*I will be loved, needed or recognised*' and we can feed off the gratitude if there is any. However, it travels with resentment and is a survival strategy from a trauma of love. Whenever tempted to rescue, other than saving a life, don't. If you feel guilty, sit with the guilt and wonder what that is about. If it is a habit of yours, monitor your habitual responses. Rescuing clients means becoming entangled with them.

Rescuer and victim survival dynamics

If a rescuer comes into relationship with someone who is adopting a victim survival attitude of helplessness and complaining, switching to self-aggrandisement or aggression, a dynamic occurs that mirrors that described by Stephen Karpman in his Drama Triangle (Karpman, 2014). The Drama Triangle represents the way a relationship can get stuck in a pattern where the two people move between the roles of rescuer, persecutor, and victim. It becomes what transactional analysis would call a 'game', the purpose of which is to avoid the true needs of both players.

Using the language of trauma theory, this is an entangled relationship between two people, both operating out of a survival strategy. Figure 5.3 shows the three survival strategies that might be used in such a dynamic. Such an entanglement is common in work and other relationships. It starts with person A (called Yvonne in this example) complaining about elements of her work – she is in her helpless victim survival mode. She may well be seen as a 'complainer' and unconsciously looks for a rescuer. Since there are many people who have rescuer as a survival strategy, there is usually someone who will respond.

We may hear similar stories told by our clients or tell them ourselves. However, despite her complaining, Yvonne doesn't really want to be rescued and rejects all suggestions that are made, other than perhaps handing over some of her work to the rescuer. This, however, doesn't stop her complaining or her sense of being a victim of some unnamed persons. The dance continues between these two survival strategies. After a while, as frustration builds, either Yvonne or her rescuer will switch into the persecutor survival strategy.

Yvonne might turn on her rescuer, blaming her for not helping and accusing her of making things worse. The rescuer will be hurt, shocked, and bewildered at this switch and has become the victim of this perpetrator survival response. Alternatively, the rescuer may switch from her survival helping and turn on Yvonne, accusing her

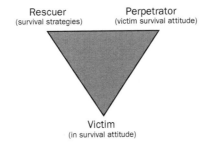

Rescuer
(survival strategies)

Perpetrator
(victim survival attitude)

Victim
(in survival attitude)

Figure 5.3 Rescuer and victim attitude dynamics

of taking up a lot of time and always complaining. Now Yvonne is the victim. As she would have been if, instead of finding a rescuer, she provoked a perpetrator, thus reaffirming a survival identity with victimhood: '*I am always a victim*'.

Furthermore, either might have turned their aggression on themselves. The rescuer might have told herself that she didn't try hard enough, or wasn't kind or skilful enough, or hadn't given Yvonne enough time and 'should have' been more generous. Yvonne might have become self-aggrandising when switching from complaining, trying to put the rescuer in her place, thus taking up a superior position.

The solution is to step out of this victim attitude: for the rescuer to explore her desire to rescue, and the links with the 'there and then', and to understand her pattern of response; for Yvonne, it is necessary for her to take responsibility for her situation and explore what healthy action is open to her.

Revenge and reconciliation

Revenge is a survival strategy. Being revengeful means continuing to be locked into the persecutor–victim dynamic. Revenge is perpetration because it involves the motivation to destroy the other person.

Seeking reconciliation can be a survival strategy if it happens at a superficial level, where the truth is avoided. Unless the perpetrator is willing to accept the pain they have caused the other, and take responsibility for their actions, there can be no reconciliation. Forgiveness can be healthy, if that forgiving means '*You did me harm that I carry to this day; I recognise that you were caught up in your own dynamics and that is for you to resolve. It is not for me to resolve it for you.*' The entanglement is broken with the healthy form of forgiveness. However, it is a survival forgiveness if it means '*I forgive you, you didn't know what you were doing*', as it carries a denial of the impact on us. The Oxford Dictionary definition of forgiveness is '*to stop feeling angry or resentful towards someone for an offence, flaw, or mistake*'. Letting go of our anger and resentfulness means that we let go of the entanglement, which is healthy, but it doesn't mean we deny the pain caused to us.

Maintaining a survival victim attitude prevents individuals taking the action they need to protect themselves. You can support clients by observing the dynamics, helping them make links with the 'there and then', coming out of the victim attitude, and deciding what is healthy for them.

If a client is a victim of perpetration in the 'here and now', you can support them in deciding what action they want to take. The same is the case for historical sexual abuse, if it is raised. Many people who were sexually abused as children do not want it to be brought to the attention of the authorities. It is a difficult decision to make because of the way people anticipate repercussions for the individual and the family. If sexual abusers are still alive, they could be continuing to abuse children. The same might be the case in an organisation in relation to bullying, victimisation, and sexual harassment. If not reported, the perpetrator may continue. Clients need to come to terms with this dilemma and you can help them decide what advice they might find helpful and from whom.

Perpetrator survival attitudes

Bullying and sexual harassment are the most common forms of perpetration in the workplace. High-performance cultures where people are driven to do more and more with fewer resources with no thanks, acknowledgement, or recognition of their personal needs, occurs where perpetration is embedded in the organisational culture. In such organisations, those who complain are seen as weak and not up to the job.

Some defend management styles of tight control over people. They will say that harsh criticism is often needed in order to get the job done. Management involves control to some extent, but it is how that is enacted that is important and over what. There are ways of providing feedback that do not involve attacking the other person. There are ways of being firm without being harsh and judgemental.

There is a tendency to pass the bullying on down the chain of command. Bullying becomes part of how things are done. Bullies justify their actions and use those justifications to avoid facing the reality of their behaviour and the impact it has on others. They cannot bully and be compassionate or empathetic: the two cannot go together. Not all bullies are alike, some consistently undermine all members of staff while others pick on certain members of staff who remind them of someone from their past. Some bully when they are feeling angry or anxious about their own circumstances.

Those who perpetrate on others do so to different degrees. At one end of the spectrum are the serial sexual perpetrators who deceive those around them, severely damaging the lives of others over many years. At the other end are people who, in response to circumstance, deploy a management style that causes harm to others or behave in sexually unacceptable ways to exert power and control over others.

Perpetrators of all degrees develop similar survival attitudes:

What clients might say	Perpetrator survival attitude
'*I don't know what the fuss is about. We have a busy workload, there are demands on all of us.*'	They don't see the harm done.
'*I have to push people to get the best out of them, to help them get results. They need to get their priorities better organised. I think they are just trying to cover up that they are not up to the job. I carry a huge responsibility and am paid to enact that and get results. The Board is very happy with me.*'	They justify their actions.

'*I am the victim here, I am the one who is moving heaven and earth to get this project finished.*'	They think of themselves as the victim.
'*She wanted me to come on to her sexually, she sent me flirty texts; she encouraged me. Yes, she is a junior member of staff, but I have done nothing she didn't want me to do and now she is afraid her boyfriend will find out.*'	They blame the victim for the perpetration enacted: '*they made me do it*'.
'*It's not true what he is saying. It didn't happen like that. He is completely over-dramatizing it. I have discussed this with senior management, and they are entirely on my side.*' – there is evidence to the contrary regarding what happened.	They deny the facts and continue to claim their power.

Serial perpetrators tend also to invest their time in 'doing good works' to hide their abuse of others. The more famous they are, and in organisational terms the more successful they are, the less likely victims will be believed, although there are signs that this is changing. Jimmy Savile, famous in the UK as a DJ and for his charitable works, is a good example of this. After his death it came to light that his involvement with charities and hospitals was a cover for committing serious sexual abuse on clients and patients within those institutions over many years.

Many clients who are accused of bullying have rationalised and normalised their behaviour. When coaching clients accused of bullying, or found to have bullied others, I take a biography as usual, listening for relevant 'there and then' experiences and invite them to share what is going on for them in work and their wider life. I ask what it feels like to be accused of this behaviour and check out their willingness to explore their capacity for self-reflection. I must remain non-judgemental and interested in their self-learning.

These are problematic contracts, as clients accused of bullying have rarely freely agreed to coaching but are attending as a condition of their 'rehabilitation'. It might be a positive attempt by the senior members of the organisation to support behaviour change or it might be focusing on one person while denying it is endemic in the organisation. Many clients 'sent' for coaching just want to get over the accusation and not change their behaviour.

The victims of bullying are often offered coaching to find a way to 'toughen up' or not 'take X so much to heart'. Coaches need to be mindful of this invitation to support bullying and the creation of survival strategies as a management style. The victim might be in survival and be unable to recognise or protect themselves from the aggression of others. Work can be done to help them, not to 'toughen them up', but to support them make healthy choices for themselves. As with all coaching, your focus should be on the healthy self of clients and what action is healthy for them.

Not all organisational cultures need to be the same and not all cultures will suit everyone. Part of our role as coaches can be to help a client move on to a culture or role that is best suited to them.

Sexual harassment is much in the news with the #metoo campaign. It is rare for those found guilty of sexual harassment to be offered coaching. However, in some circumstances they might be, particularly if found it was a 'one-off' event, and the harasser had a previously good record. Here a coach describes a client offered coaching after sexually harassing a colleague:

> '*J was offered coaching after being found guilty of sexual harassment. He was in shock about what had happened and felt angry at how it had been handled. He started off blaming the victim and justifying himself. He was open to coaching and to self-exploration. It transpired that he was very lonely, having recently divorced, and had taken the behaviour of the other as an invitation for closeness. We explored how she might have felt by his behaviour that led to her reporting him and what his motivation had been. We looked at the power dynamics as he was her boss. He came to understand how he had got himself into that situation, at a time when he felt vulnerable. He felt ashamed. I admired him for his willingness to face up to it all.*'

The above example illustrates the steps that need to be taken when working with people identified as 'perpetrators'. First, they must be willing participants in the coaching process. They need to have enough healthy self available to them for self-reflection and self-responsibility. The coach could talk of bullying or sexual harassment as survival responses and use the 'split in the psyche' model if it is felt appropriate. The exploration of what is happening to clients emotionally in their current life helps identify deeper stimuli for the behaviour. Clients need to empathise with their 'victim' and be helped to understand the impact of their behaviour on them. Part of this is to withdraw the blame from the other and coaches may need to challenge perpetrator survival attitudes. The final step is to be able to take self-responsibility for one's actions. This may be accompanied by shame, regret, and other emotions. There may be a desire for retribution and in relation to this the coach can explore the what, how, when, and why? Sometimes the perpetrator directs their energy inwards, via self-criticism, self-hatred, a lack of compassion for themselves, and abuse of their body through drinking too much, a poor diet, or getting too little sleep.

The perpetrator–victim dynamic is one of the lasting legacies of trauma (Figure 5.4). At its heart are the cut-off trauma feelings.

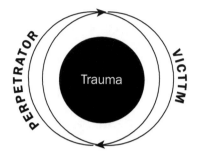

Figure 5.4 Victim, perpetrator, and trauma

We need to be careful as coaches that we are not invited in to perpetrate on a client on behalf of their organisation, as when asked to '*sort John/Jane out*'. This can occur when a manager has failed to deal with an employee and their performance in a healthy way and offers them coaching as a means of '*being seen to do the right thing*' before moving them out of the team, or where the employee is a convenient scapegoat for wider problems in the department. This is like disruptive children in families being identified as 'the problem' when it is a family systems issue. It enables the department or family to be in denial.

If we seek to please the person who commissioned the coaching or demonstrate our effectiveness, this can lead us to take on work assignments that involve us in victim and perpetrator dynamics. If we want to rescue the commissioner of coaching or the client, we can also fail to pay attention to what is being asked and why. We might also end up wanting to perpetrate on the client, if they are annoying or irritating, and find ourselves in agreement with the boss that the client is indeed the problem.

Your responsibility as a coach is to look to yourself and your own perpetrator–victim dynamics. This involves self-reflection following client sessions, and in your life generally. It is important to bring your unconscious stimuli into conscious awareness where you can explore them. If you find yourself in a 'poor me' place of victim survival attitude, notice it and decide what you want. Take action that is healthy for yourself. If you notice you carry perpetrator energy towards a specific client, explore what is going on for you. Who has this client become for you? What is the dynamic that is operating between you and in you? This is where supervision can be so valuable, as it helps to reflect with another.

Clients who demonstrate the perpetrator–victim and rescuer dynamics in their narratives can be helped to understand these as survival responses, and to explore what the stimuli are for the behaviour. You can map out clients' behaviour using the survival dynamics played out in these three positions. You can offer psyche education about victim survival attitudes and those of perpetrators. You can challenge these when you hear them and normalise them. You can adopt rescuing as a survival strategy.

With clients who have a larger trauma biography, you will feel the perpetrator–victim dynamics in relationship with them. Your challenge is not to get caught up in your own perpetrator-victim survival responses but to stay grounded in your healthy self.

Supervision, conducted with a supervisor or peer group, is the best place to explore these dynamics. Supervision can provide a safe space to role-play about how to respond to a client adopting victim or perpetrator survival attitudes and how to introduce models that might be of help.

Some clients might be helped by exploring non-violent communication ideas and practice (www.nvc-uk.com). This helps to strengthen the voice of the healthy self when dealing with conflict or interpersonal problems and avoid reverting to the perpetrator–victim survival dynamics. If we want to change our habitual 'there and then' responses to triggers in the 'here and now', understanding them has to be the first step. The next steps are investing in some personal work to reset the pathways through new practices and addressing our own trauma. This is true of both coaches and clients.

Entangled relationships

All relationships in the present are vulnerable to the replay of our earliest relationship dynamics. The trauma of love and trauma of sexuality result in survival attachment and dependency behaviour in relationships as adults.

The idea of entangled or co-dependent relationships describes unhealthy dynamics in relationship. The entanglement typically involves the survival self of

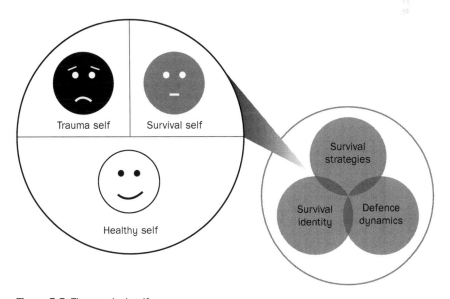

Figure 5.5 The survival self

Source: Adapted from Franz Ruppert (2012).

one person becoming locked into the survival self of another – for example, the rescuer and victim attitude described earlier, or where a victim is entangled with a perpetrator, or a needy survival self is caught up in a dependency dynamic with someone whose survival is about fostering that neediness.

Such an entanglement may only take one session to arise, when our survival self becomes entangled with the survival self in the client. It could also happen if the trauma self and feelings of clients emerge in a session and coaches respond in survival mode. These are episodes in the relationship and can be reflected on afterwards.

Deeper problems emerge when entanglement or co-dependency defines the relationship. Many of the examples I gave earlier in this chapter illustrate such relationships. The perpetrator, victim, and rescuer survival attitudes are embedded in entangled relationship, where the survival selves become entangled.

Entangled or co-dependent relationships arise from deep fears of not being wanted, loved, or protected, of being abandoned and alone. People may constantly seek approval from others or use idealisation to deny the rounded reality of the other. There may be a deep fear of failure and shame. Faux-independence may be used to defend against a deep fear of dependency. Healthy autonomy is sacrificed and replaced by adaptive, insecure attachment behaviour.

The relationships clients bring into coaching are likely to be entangled relationships, otherwise they would not be causing difficulties. Most of the coaching relationships that feel unsatisfactory are entangled. Coaches can become entangled with those who sponsor coaching and establish a co-dependency relationship.

Unconsciously, clients may set out to entangle us in different ways. It is our responsibility to observe, understand, and avoid any such invitation. It is also important coaches do not give out entanglement invitations to clients (including sponsors). For example:

> 'I started to meet Y (the client) for coffee before the session, at her request, and that felt okay. We have a pattern now. She says she likes having the social connection and that she can find out about me. I want her to like me as she can recommend me to others. I didn't feel I could refuse and now I can't get out of it.'

> 'I really want to help G. He seems stuck in such a difficult place. I have asked him to email me whenever he needs to and I will respond. In the sessions he is quite reserved, and It feels that I do most of the work, I suppose, but I really want to help and to be seen to be a good coach.'

In the first of these the client initiated the entanglement, in the second the coach did. We see the desire to be liked, which overrides thoughts about boundaries and social space. Entanglement also results if there is a desire to fill up the space left by a client's non-involvement, from a fear of being seen as a failure:

> *'C finds it hard to engage with the coaching, so I suggest the exercises we do and give him homework. He then responds, so I think it is helping. This is the first client I have had from this company and I really want it to be successful.'*

We might also find that we are joining in with a distraction because we enjoy it and it enables us to avoid tackling the behaviour:

> *'The client likes winding me up. I respond jokingly and we have a lot of banter. This does distract from the coaching, but I enjoy our meetings. I do worry that the coaching isn't really progressing though.'*

Co-dependency may mean giving up what is good for the coach and for the coaching, in a desire for recognition, being liked and valued. Coaches might also be seeking more work with the organisation and the chance to work with more senior and 'important' people, or perhaps to move beyond coaching into broader organisational consulting. This may result in a conflict between the needs of the presenting client and those of the sponsoring client funding the coaching on behalf of the organisation.

Clients will talk of relationships in which they are 'going the extra mile' for the other person for little reward, or how important it is to them that they manage the relationship in a particular way, or don't see or fear the perpetrator and want to get closer to them. The narratives might show a clinging dependency on a person, job, or organisation, where the fear is that the individual cannot survive without that person, job, or organisation. This makes it very hard, if not impossible, to end the relationship. Working ever harder at a relationship also implies dependency, with the unfilled hope for recognition and love.

There may be indications of feeling easily abandoned, for example, *'The client hasn't come back to me and I am afraid he is not going to. I'm worried that maybe I said or did something he didn't like, I think I will give him a call to check.'* Relationships might be defined by the need for approval or being noticed, and a willingness to jump through hoops in the hope of that outcome. There could be an identification or idealisation: *'You are so wonderful; I want to be just like you'*; or, *'I really admire him, he has achieved so much, I can't imagine what I can offer really that will be of value.'*

Entanglement might be around control and submission. Here, a person is looking to be submissive, to have decisions made for them, and finding someone who thrives when controlling others. Or vice versa. Feelings of guilt or resentment give clues about rescuing, as do stories of self-sacrifice. Such relationships sacrifice healthy autonomy because of the links with the 'there and then'. As infants we desire symbiosis with our mother or primary caregiver. There is no sense of being separate beings. As infants develop, they also want autonomy, claiming themselves as separate from the other. Think of the toddler saying 'no', 'won't', 'mine'.

Where this move to autonomy is successfully negotiated between mother and child, children develop a sense of connection with themselves and a confidence that being themselves, being separate, does not threaten the intimacy and love with the primary caregiver. We can have the symbiotic intimacy without giving up on the individuation of our healthy self. Where this is not successfully negotiated, the early relationships become entangled, as children learn that their individuation is not welcome and threatens their attachment.

In healthy autonomy, we know what we want for ourselves, for our well-being. The following example is of a client who recognised how she might have habitually responded and decided to take action that was healthy for herself:

> 'It felt like a real achievement. I could feel myself thinking I should submit to the hostile criticism she was directing towards me, and I could feel my anxiety rising. But instead of being submissive as I always have been in the past, I just said, "I am going, as I am not in the right space to listen to this now," and just left.'

In a place of healthy autonomy, we know and act on what is healthy for us. We can attach to others without entanglement, we can break those attachments when they stop being healthy. We have a sense of our self-worth. We don't need to adapt to meet the needs or perceived needs of others, or to protect ourselves from rejection or abandonment.

Even with the concept of healthy autonomy we must be careful of a survival version as we seek to come out of unhealthy relationships. The survival versions are faux-autonomy, they are about being strong and independent, not needing anyone else, out of a fear of dependency, or dominating others to protect our vulnerability about dependency. Faux-autonomy also includes striving to be perfect so no one can criticise us, being rebellious, not seeking or accepting help. Sometimes people are labelled as 'strong' by others as a survival projection; and we might come to identify with that which means we have to keep any vulnerability well hidden. This is not healthy autonomy but is often disguised to look like it.

Where there is faux-autonomy, there is a fear of being 'swallowed up' by the other, of losing a sense of separateness. The relationships made from this survival self tend to be those that are on 'my terms only'. We choose separateness over intimacy, not realising that we can be in an intimate or close relationship and still retain a sense of our separateness. From healthy autonomy we can ask for help when we need it and we can accept that help when given to us; we can be intimate and not lose ourselves.

Stepping out of entanglement

The first step is to recognise that you are in an entangled or co-dependent relationship. Entangled coaching relationships should be explored in supervision, to reflect on your part in them, finding how to let it go and step back into your healthy self.

In the box below, there are some examples of how entanglements may appear between coach and client:

Client / Coach	Healthy self	Survival self	Trauma self
Healthy self	Non-entangled; each operating from healthy autonomy. Coaching is effective and personal change is possible.	The coach avoids getting caught up in the client's survival self-invitations to entanglement. The coach does not get caught in the perpetrator–victim and rescuer dynamics.	The coach can bear being with the client in touch with his traumatised feelings without moving into her survival self and strategies. She can offer empathetic support.
Survival self	The coach wants to entangle the client by rescuing, controlling, creating dependence, perpetrating, being distant. The client avoids this invitation and is unlikely to continue the coaching contract.	Both are entangled. The process will be dysfunctional without much progress, insight or change. The perpetrator–victim dynamics will be present, as will other characteristics of entangled relationship.	The coach is unable to bear the pain experienced by the client and can only offer 'faux-compassion'; more likely to try to shut down the trauma self and/or to become more overly directive. May find she is critical of the client afterwards. No coaching is possible.
Trauma self	The client will see or sense the vulnerable state of the coach and that he is not able to do effective work. The client will pull away or offer empathetic support.	There can be no useful contact between the coach and the client. The coach has no contact with her healthy self resources in that moment and may feel victimised by the client.	Neither can attend to the other. There can be no coaching and no relationship. Neither are likely to attend the planned session.

Adapted from Ruppert (2012).

In the following example, the coach and client are entangled:

> *'I find this client very difficult, she keeps going on and on about things that don't seem relevant to what she said she wanted to work on. I feel caught in her stuff. It has always been like this, I've been working with her for over a year. She just takes over. It makes me very frustrated, I think she just doesn't want to do the coaching. I am going to suggest we end or find a way of ending it.'*

This coach is judging the client and is showing elements of a victim survival attitude. However, the two of them have been locked in this dance for a while. Instead of ending it, the coach can ask herself questions we can all ask when we realise we are entangled:

> *'What is going on? What happens to me at the beginning, during, and the end of the session? What do I do and what am I feeling?'*

> *'What needs of mine are being inappropriately invested in this relationship?'*

> *'What was in the contracting? Did I go through what coaching means in terms of self-enquiry? If not, why not? Did I avoid something in the coaching contracting process, and if so, what was happening for me?'*

> *'Might I be entangled with the sponsoring organisation? Is there a form of co-dependency in operation? Do we depend on each other for professional survival?'*

> *'What is the client coming for? Is this clear and is it coaching? If it isn't for coaching, why am I doing it?'*

> *'What am I avoiding? What is not being addressed? Within me and the relationship?'*

Since 'here and now' relationships can mirror those of 'there and then', it can be a useful exercise for you to explore *'Who has this person become for me? Was it the parent or sibling I was desperate to please or afraid of? Is it someone who took advantage of me as a child?'* If you can gain insight into your own projections, you are better able to understand your responses and free yourselves from the survival entanglement.

- You can help those clients who wish to gain an understanding of the entanglement dynamics and step out of them.
- You can explain about survival self, strategies, and dynamics, and that relationships in the present can replay those from 'there and then' in terms of our unconscious needs, wants, and fears.

- You can set out the dynamics and explore what feelings are evoked by the behaviour of the other and lie behind the client's behaviour; you can work at a feelings level.
- You can talk about healthy autonomy and the healthy self-resources.
- You can ask what would be healthier for the client? What do they want?

Entanglements are deeply embedded as a way of relating, therefore any elements of self-awareness are valuable, as is learning how to break a specific entanglement at work. Being able to come out of entanglement as a 'habitual' response will take time and involve personal therapy work.

You have to be sure that, as far as is possible, we are in a place of healthy autonomy in respect of our clients. That means managing your boundaries, respecting your needs, respecting the differences in the other, asking permission of the other regarding inviting exploration, being clear in your expectations and what you can't offer, and taking your survival self out of the relationship.

6   Trauma, leadership, and teams

The splits in the psyche have implications for leadership and teams. In this chapter, I explore some of the implications of trauma for leadership and the survival dynamics in teams.

Traumatised leaders, with a predominant survival self, are likely to create traumatising cultures for their staff. Traumatised followers, managing their work and career through their survival self, are vulnerable to becoming entangled with such leaders. Leadership is ultimately a product of the relationship between those with 'leader' in their role brief, or who take up leadership, and those who are followers within the context in which they find themselves. Such relationships are open to the survival dynamics of entanglement, perpetration, and victim dynamics and survival strategies in the same ways as any other relationship. What makes the leader–follower relationship important is the unequal distribution of power. The power is conferred on the leader. This is similar to the case with children, where the power lies with the parent(s) and adults in the family or community.

Leadership can stimulate feelings of vulnerability. Being 'the leader' can be lonely, with many expectations and hopes projected onto the role holder. The role can stimulate fears, for example, of being watched, of envy, of rejection, and of letting people down, including the internalised parents or grandparents with whom they may have identified with. Taking on a leadership role often means a steep learning curve with associated fears of failure and costly errors. It can stimulate associations with early experience, together with an increase in stress and anxiety levels. This is to be expected and is familiar territory for coaches and leadership developers.

There are other expressions of the surviving self that mean people are less likely to access coaching. Consequently, coaches are most likely to meet the followers who experience the work relationship and work context as difficult, and who have become entangled with it.

Some leaders will have gained their leadership role through predominant survival self-behaviour and decision-making. They may have achieved professional success and be highly regarded because of that. However, the survival self will include the victim and perpetrator dynamics that harm both the individual and others. The survival strategies are likely to include those of addiction, control, and denial. Dominant survival behaviour is often deeply entrenched by the time the individual is in a senior position.

Sometimes, these survival self-patterns backfire. Individuals may make serious misjudgements or errors. Sometimes the lack of rest associated with such an inner structure leads to lack of sleep, exhaustion, and burnout, with the need to leave work. In the example of Bruce, below, told by his coach, it was a serious misjudgement that brought him to coaching:

> 'Bruce had been sacked in a very public manner from his job as director of a high-profile company. He was shocked by this and after a while came to coaching. Until his dismissal he had been very successful. He really understood his business and had a strategic vision for what was needed. However, he crossed a line with his CEO, and not for the first time.
>
> 'He wanted to move forward and was willing to explore his role in what had happened. He felt very mistreated and angry. He recognised his survival strategies of work addiction, control, and demanding perfection. He found it harder to recognise survival responses of self-aggrandisement; however, he recognised he had overplayed his hand. He was able to take on that he had driven staff hard, but was unable to go further than that.
>
> 'Exploring the "there and then" in the "here and now", he made connections with the traumatising conditions of his childhood. His desire to be successful come what may was a response to feeling deeply unsafe.
>
> 'He had enough healthy self to engage with this process and was able to explore what would be healthier for him from now on. However, while he had recognised some of his survival strategies, I suggested to him that therapy might be useful to work with the early material which he had never told anyone else about before. Without that I thought the survival behaviours would return as soon as he was back in work.'

Not many clients who have shown such predominant survival behaviour as Bruce, above, may be as open to exploring their behaviour and its impact on others. As with all coaching, we can only work with the available healthy self in the client and limit the activation of our own survival responses. The coach is correct in his view that, unless Bruce does therapeutic work, his survival responses will return. While we can recognise survival behaviour from the healthy self, only lasting change will be achieved by engaging with the feelings that it is designed to block.

Follower dispositions can fit into such survival personalities like a jigsaw. The follower with a 'dependent' surviving self, for example, who avoids making decisions from fear of getting it wrong, and through trying to please the parent, will fit nicely but unhealthily into an entangled relationship with someone who likes to control. Those leaders who survive by depression may attract followers who like to rescue, perhaps like they used to rescue their parents who were depressed. Leaders who bully may attract those who think they can appease perpetrators, not recognising them to be the dangerous person they are.

The other survival self-dynamic common among people in senior leadership roles is that of narcissism. We all need some healthy narcissism to progress in the world, to be able to believe that the world needs us. Unfortunately, it can also be a robust survival strategy. As such, it is a complex combination of:

Perpetrator energy	. . . destroying those they envy, by controlling, bullying, undermining, being ambitious, seeking and claiming power.
Illusions	. . . about their own ability, seeing themselves as brilliant, always successful.
Grandiosity	. . . being more important than anyone else, even the company; their own work is the most important.
Denial	. . . that their behaviour has any negative impact on anyone else, and that if it does, it doesn't matter.
A lack of capacity for empathy or compassion	. . . for others or themselves.

Despite this complexity, such people are often considered successful, and their unacceptable behaviour is tolerated and goes unchallenged.

There is a tendency to use labels such as 'narcissist', 'sociopath', or 'paranoid' when describing strongly presenting survival dynamics. I caution you to be careful about labelling your clients in this way, as you are attributing to them an identity. It is better to talk of someone using, for example, a narcissistic survival strategy or expressing paranoid thoughts. This separates the person from the behaviour and leaves space for the healthy self to emerge. It breaks the identification. If coaching anyone working for someone who uses narcissistic or other persecutory survival strategies, the risk is that your client will find ways of adapting to their demands. They may sacrifice themselves through an illusion of job security or denial that '*it is not that bad*', when all the evidence suggests to you that it is just so. It will usually be better for the client to find another job and another boss.

In the following example, Sonia works for such a boss:

> '*Sonia believed she could help her boss and felt he had a good side, even though he treated her badly. She worked late, she took on extra work, she lost a lot of her private life and her relationship was troubled. To survive, she started to use bullying as a survival strategy. This led to her downfall, in a very painful, distressing and confusing way.*'

If Sonia has sufficient access to her healthy self and to her resources for self-enquiry, coaching can help her recognise this as an entanglement with the boss and the job. Some connections might be possible with the 'there and then', which are likely to have a connection with her deep fears of abandonment and her other trauma feelings. We don't need to rescue or reassure, but instead to be present with her feelings. By this process she may be able to talk about what would be healthy for her, which might include therapy. However, if access to her healthy self is limited, the likelihood of successful coaching will also be limited.

The example of Joseph, below, shows him using victim survival attitudes to protect his boss, and attempting to resolve the situation by developing more robust survival strategies:

> 'Joseph came to coaching because he was increasingly unhappy at work and because his boss said she was unhappy with his performance. When talking about that relationship he was always protective of Kate, his boss, saying she didn't mean it, she was under stress, she meant well. Kate regularly required him to stay at work late and to come in very early for breakfast meetings at 7.30 am. Joseph had a distressing family problem which he shared with Kate, who laughed and was dismissive. Joseph blamed himself for raising it. He said he learnt so much from Kate, who he said really understood the business. Joseph's goal for coaching was to be "more efficient", to be able to get through more work, and to be a "better support" to Kate.'

Joseph is entangled with his boss and is setting survival goals for the coaching. It is up to him whether he is able to face the truth of this relationship, to let go of the idealisation of Kate, and to explore what would be healthier for him. If he can do that, it is likely that finding another job would be seen as a priority. The only future for this relationship is likely to be one of continued perpetration and entanglement.

People with predominant survival selves, particularly those with the complex dynamics of narcissism or who use behaviour sometimes referred to as 'psychopathic' – that is, with apparently little conscience and misusing relationships for their own end – can be difficult to lead. The power dynamics do not influence their behaviour – they do not want to 'please' the boss or to 'fit in'. Individuals who are narcissistic will put their ambitions above those of the team, boss, and organisation. Others with more psychopathic survival behaviour may be able to get the admiration of many, while delivering nothing much of value because of their grandiosity and lack of commitment to collective goals. They are likely to see work as being less important than their own perceived success.

The example below involves a manager discussing a member of staff whose survival behaviour is a combination of narcissism and manipulation:

> 'I feel like it is all smoke and mirrors. When I meet Ben, he tells me all is going well; yes, the projects are on course, there are some difficulties

but they are due to a third party and he is sorting it. When I look though, nothing seems to be happening. When I challenged him, he told a colleague, who came and told me I should stop picking on Ben. I didn't think I was. I thought he was a great appointment, he came from an organisation I thought well of and had an important role there. I have just learnt from a colleague in that organisation that they also had problems with him.'

There is an invitation from people such as Ben to become entangled, for his boss to get angry and persecutory, for example by actually picking on Ben. The boss might take back some of the work out of frustration and concern, and overload himself. Ben is unlikely to change and much more likely to move on. The issue for this client is how to prevent becoming entangled and to find a response from his healthy self. He needs to use performance management procedures fairly, and with clear evidence. The client needs his own organisational support, or it is possible that Ben may become persecutory of the client, who could come out of it badly.

Those with such a complex survival structure are deeply traumatised individuals, who rarely access coaching, because they do not think they need it. However, they might if they 'have to' as part of a leadership programme, although tend to do so without really connecting with the process. However, such a survival dynamic usually results in major self-destruction, for example, by overestimating their own ability, taking a risk too far and making a serious mistake. Then they might access coaching and may need therapy as their survival self is so broken that old strategies no longer work.

The response of many leaders and those being led who are surviving in this way is to become entangled, and to rely on survival dynamics, to ensure deeper trauma feelings are suppressed. People who find they are working for someone with a narcissistic survival self will likely feel bullied, yet may also be desperate to please. They may adopt a rescuer survival pattern, thinking they can save the other, as they may have tried to do with one of their parents when they were a child. It is an opportunity for such clients, if they wish, to explore their survival self and strategies, to make the links with their past, and to access their healthy self so they can decide what is healthy for them.

Imposter syndrome is another well-documented way in which the survival self might show itself. In some ways, this syndrome is in total contrast to the narcissist dynamic. We often meet this in coaching, as clients who use it as a survival strategy believe they need coaching to improve because they *'are simply not good enough'*, despite all the evidence to the contrary. Such clients may have identified with messages they picked up on as children, or they may be protecting their parents by not being more successful than them, or they may be fearful of envy, again possibly historically as a result of family experience. The internalised ideas are, *'I am not as good as people think I am'* and *'It is dangerous to stand out (I will be attacked)'*. This survival-self blocks any internalisation of positive feedback and might go into self-attack if something has gone well, as in the example of Naomi below, as told by her coach:

> 'Naomi always has very good feedback, people seem to like her and value her. Every talk she gives attracts rave reviews, but Naomi always berates herself for not getting it right in her view. She discounts such feedback, saying, "what do they know?" After one successful event she reported being unable to sleep as she felt so agitated and disturbed and the next day plunged into a process of deep self-annihilation. When challenged she said to me, "I felt so frightened that someone would come up and tell me I had got things wrong".'

This destructive inner part of the survival self destroys our creativity and any feelings of success and achievement. This is the internalised conflation of critical early figures, and an identification with them. Marion Woodman, the Jungian therapist and writer, called this process the 'death mother'. In her book, *Understanding and Healing Emotional Trauma* (2015), Sieff describes Woodman's concept of the death mother as being a physiological as well as emotional process of collapse, resulting from a deep feeling of terror, with life energy draining away. It is a survival response to not being loved or feeling our parents or teachers found us unacceptable. It blocks off access to our autonomy and agency. It is a very persecutory inner part of us.

As coaches, we can work with this in several ways. For example, we can look at the functionality of the response:

> 'I asked Naomi, "Suppose you are as good as everyone tells you you are, what would that mean?" She replied, "I find that very hard to contemplate. I just know it isn't true. I would get lazy and arrogant. I think I'm lazy as it is".'

This is a survival self-response. The coach will need to be sure the client wants to explore her reactions and these inner dynamics, as a survival response could indicate there may not be a willingness to do so. The coach may need to find other ways to engage the healthy self.

If permitted to do so, we can offer our own observation, for example: '*I notice how hard it is for you to allow yourself to feel successful*', or '*I notice how you attack yourself when you do something well in public*'. This is talking to the healthy self.

We can invite such clients to map their mood and emotions when they have done something well, in terms of the consistency of the feedback that tells them so. Naomi's map is shown in Figure 6.1. Here is Naomi talking about this map:

> 'I felt quite excited about the event, but I had no time for myself beforehand or after. I was with people, which was very nice, but I think it

contributed to what happened. I was quite anxious, I hadn't run it before. When I reflected afterwards, I realised that I had become anxious in the afternoon and I didn't handle part of it as well as I wanted, although the participants didn't appear to think that. I dwelt on that and then thought of all the bits that could have been so much better. I had to push that to one side for the evening with friends, but at night it all came back. It took me days to get back to some normality.'

The process of mapping allowed Naomi to explore the survival responses and the triggers, her fears of being rejected/criticised. It led her to think about how she might set things up another time, which might allow her not to slip into the survival pattern. When the healthy self is activated in this way, we can explore connections with the 'there and then', if the client so wishes. This will not prevent the terror arising again but will enable Naomi to change some of the conditions to make her less vulnerable to it.

People who use this way of surviving early trauma tend to keep themselves in the middle of organisations or as second in commands where they can be vulnerable to entanglements with the boss. They may also find themselves occupying a training, internal consulting, or human resources role. If they do get the top post, the fear of not living up to expectations (the expectations of their parents, teachers, significant others, for example) will be high, which produces demanding expectations of self and others with potential bullying and controlling dynamics. For those with such patterns, 360-degree feedback can be very challenging and needs handling with great care.

Individuals who lead through a predominant survival self have an unhealthy impact on those around them. They may be deemed to be 'very successful' in terms

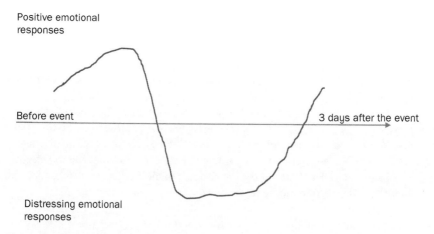

Figure 6.1 The timeline of Naomi's emotional responses

of financial gain or business impact. Some may be idealised by the system, rarely though by those who work for them, but they are forgiven for their bad behaviour by others because, *'They really know their stuff'*, or *'They really put the hours in; what commitment'*. They rarely show emotional intelligence and drive themselves and others very hard.

Leader–follower relationships can become very entangled. When that is the case, the depth of the entanglement makes it difficult for the followers to leave, however great the demands on them might be. They have no access to their healthy autonomy and are stuck with perpetrator and victim attitudes and survival anxiety.

Traumatised leaders with perpetration dynamics create traumatising or 'toxic' organisations. Such organisations have a culture of covert or overt bullying, with associated high levels of controlling and belittling behaviour. Scapegoating occurs in the guise of strong performance management. There is minimal tolerance of performance that doesn't meet expectations. This stimulates hypervigilance and the exacerbation of survival defence behaviour, as the trauma feelings are so provoked. Employees of such organisations often deploy work addiction as part of the entanglement, with its associated impact on their personal lives. Such organisations do not give value to the personal lives of employees, in fact they are seen as part of the problem for the organisation. There are high costs to personal and private lives. The perpetrator energy might also be present in a highly competitive environment and/or aggressive takeovers.

Such organisations do not respect boundaries and may seek to blur public and private space. They may expect employees to access work emails and take and make work phone calls from home. They will also be expected to do a lot of work in 'home' time. Even if this is not explicitly requested, employees can fail to protect their own boundaries. Trauma has a negative impact on boundary management, either through perpetration on the boundaries of others, the inability to protect our own boundaries, or both.

Because of this denial of the 'personal' being outside the control of the perpetrator, there is likely to be discrimination against employees who are parents, with parental responsibilities being ignored or dismissed as something that employees have to get sorted. No organisational support is given to parents or those with other carer responsibilities. It is an unempathetic and uncompassionate environment. Absenteeism is seen as a failure or lack of commitment.

The survival strategies that are stimulated within employees will be addictions, denial, and illusion. They will be entangled with the organisation. Burnout, depression, and stress-related illnesses are likely. Relationships may break down, leading to separation and divorce. Such organisations can have profound effects on the children of those caught up in these dynamics.

We need to be sure that we do not collude or become entangled with such organisations. They are damaging to health and well-being. When working with clients who are entangled, we can help them come to see that for themselves through supporting their healthy self.

The impact of traumatising leaders is the reason why leadership development needs to include a focus on personal growth, self-awareness, and emotional intelligence. If leaders wish to become good leaders, in the widest sense, they need to dig deep into their inner psychology and unpick elements of the survival self and do work with their trauma feelings, so they do not pass on their trauma to others.

Some occupational contexts are re-traumatising due to the nature of the work, for example, disaster relief work, aspects of medicine, military conflicts, the rescue services, and the police. Many such occupational areas have protocols for supporting those who are affected by the shocking situations they come across in the line of duty. Others may be re-traumatised even if they are not caught up in the life-threatening events themselves. When coaching individuals in these occupational areas, it helps to be aware of the potential impact of the nature of the work on their intra-psyche dynamics – that is, on the interplay between the environment and the splits in the psyche. This is the case with medicine, for example, where the pressure is intense, life and death decisions need to be made, and mistakes can have catastrophic consequences.

Resilience is often seen as the capacity to 'bounce back', to be able to absorb pressure in a healthy way, through self-regulation and lack of entanglement. Without resilience, we become hyperstressed, exhausted, and anxious, which may result in long absences from work. In relation to the traumatised psyche, resilience is a product of the healthy self. It is the ability to be healthily autonomous, to avoid getting entangled or caught up with the perpetrator–victim dynamics. Where the capacity for resilience is limited, or absent, there may be an underlying identity trauma and subsequent trauma biography. The survival self is uppermost in behaviour and life choices intended to limit the internal pain. We can build up our resilience by learning about our survival strategies and how to provide more space for our healthy self. We need also to learn and use self-regulation processes to keep our stress levels within normal limits. Many people need to learn to do this in adulthood, as they were unable to develop the capacity for self-regulation in childhood.

As stated in earlier chapters, there is a spectrum across which survival selves and strategies are predominant (see Figure 6.2). Traumatised leaders may be at any point on this spectrum. The nearer they are to the right-hand side, the more they are open to coaching. The nearer they are to the left-hand side, coaching is less likely to impact on behaviour change. If there is a personal crisis, appropriate trauma therapy is probably a better solution.

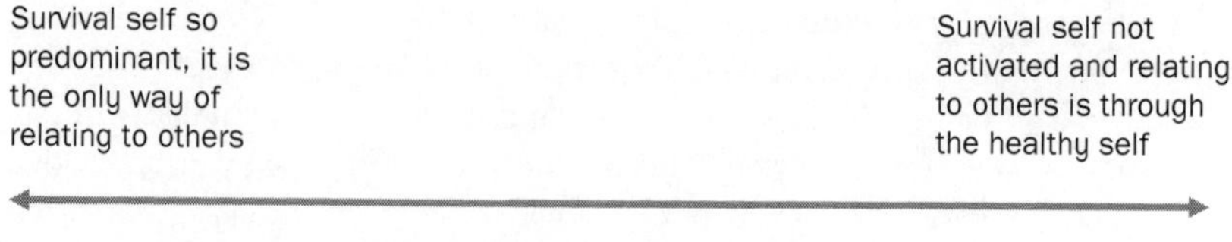

Survival self so predominant, it is the only way of relating to others

Survival self not activated and relating to others is through the healthy self

Figure 6.2 Spectrum of survival self-predominance in relationships

Traumatised teams

Teams can become traumatised through the collective team members' responses to events, bringing a range of survival dynamics into play. The causal factors may be a shared exposure to an existential trauma such as fire, terrorist attack or war, or other threats to life from the nature of the work. Such team members are sometimes referred to as an *adversity group*, as they share the same life-threatening experience. Such teams often need specialised help to process their collective experience. They also become traumatised as a result of a set of organisational events that have a profound impact on all team members and their capacity to continue to do their work collectively. Whatever the cause, those individuals already traumatised by earlier life experience are more likely to be affected than those whose trauma biography is less intense.

Here, I focus on teams in organisations that are subject to a set of circumstances which have a profound emotional impact on all team members, their wellbeing, and their capacity to do their work collectively. I do not address occupations where the lives of team members are at risk. Coaches are often asked to coach the leaders of such teams, or people who have been parachuted in to '*get this team back together*' or to '*sort them out*'. We also find ourselves coaching individuals who are members of such teams. Managing, and being part of, teams that are traumatised is a considerable challenge because of the survival dynamics and the history that has brought them to where they now are.

Characteristics of traumatised teams

A team of people who come together around a collective task or purpose have a shared sense of identity. There are established ways of holding the individuals together around the task, and members are held in that role relationship by managerial and organisational structures. In traumatising circumstances, the individual team members' trauma feelings, such as fear of abandonment, attachment loss, vulnerability, shame and rage are activated, and therefore also their survival responses. These survival responses can be both individual and collective in nature. The metaphorical 'psyche' of the team is split in the same way as for individuals. The survival responses will limit the capacity for self-reflection, for talking calmly about feelings and needs, and the amount of respect and compassion felt for others. The capacity for trust between individual team members, and between team members and management will be damaged. There will also be anger as a defence against feeling vulnerable and hurt.

How does a traumatised team present? When managers are your clients, they will talk of feeling being kept at a distance by team members while also being subject to anger and criticism at every opportunity. They may feel overwhelmed and angry, wanting to punish the team members. It is likely they don't understand what is happening and that everything they try falls on deaf ears. They find it almost impossible to harness followership.

You may hear clients talk about the team members being collectively angry and rude to them, that communication is poor, with no responses to emails and/or phone calls. Clients may describe the existence of subgroups with power-bases and no collective willingness to come together to resolve the problems voiced or to explore what is going on. They are aware of a lot of unhappiness being expressed in the team.

Traumatised team members tend to place the blame for their experience outside the team, focusing on management, or create a scapegoat within the team. Team members perpetrate on these others and justify their behaviour. The illusion is that if only the scapegoat were to go, all would be fine. Alongside all this, because team working has broken down, small or large mistakes occur, which only add to the lack of safety felt by the team.

Clients who are managers may face the dilemma of staying and sorting things out or leaving as quickly as possible. They, too, distance themselves as protection and draw on their survival strategies. They often feel unsupported by the organisational hierarchy and may be pressured from above to punish the team. The following example is of a sub-directorate manager talking about what is happening within their team:

> 'I don't know what to do. Everything I try is rejected. The work goes on, but it feels like a tinder box. Staff meetings are dreadful, full of accusations and anger. I'm not sleeping because of the worry about it all.

A team member might describe their experience as follows:

> 'The management is useless, they have no concern about us at all. We are all doing the best we can and yet they keep on at us as if we have done something wrong. It is they who have done it all. We have suffered one thing after another, we are being persecuted. I am so stressed out, I am very afraid I will make a mistake, I am not sleeping; I don't know what to do.'

It is possible that this team member is part of a team led by someone with strong perpetrator survival strategies. However the focus of coaching is the same, supporting the client identify what is healthy for him and what he can take self-responsibility for. If he is a victim of the manager, he may additionally be operating from his victim survival attitudes.

The concept of traumatised teams can help us to understand the dynamics where there are other factors other than having a manager who is a perpetrator.

Such factors are usually cumulative and become the 'trauma biography' of the team. One factor alone is unlikely to be re-traumatising. The event responsible for the most trauma survival responses is usually preceded by several other events that disturbed the team's equanimity, attachments, and identity.

In high-risk occupations such as health care, errors can have serious consequences for the life or health of others. Such events are shocking and deeply disturbing to the team dynamics. Ongoing investigations after a major incident are often experienced as punitive and persecutory so are unlikely to reassure or calm the group. If, however, there is enough trust, support for individual members, and opportunities to talk about what has happened and the effect on the team, the impact on team dynamics can by minimised.

Whenever I have been asked to work with teams and leaders of teams in crisis, as a coach my survival self was provoked, and in some cases I became entangled. I allowed myself to get sucked in: to want to be the 'heroic rescuer'; to feel and be rejected; to feel hopeless and helpless, and to use analysis and 'intellectual exploration' as survival strategies. In this way, through my survival self, there was some identification with the group, and I was able to feel the transference of their emotional responses. In my defence, I also listened, witnessed, acknowledged, clarified, supported, and did my level best to stick to my role brief. I mention my failures in order to highlight the strength of these team dynamics and the need for pairing with another consultant/coach, or good supervision with a colleague, when working such team trauma.

Survival dynamics of traumatised teams

As with individuals, the extent to which teams retain access to a 'healthy self', and the extent to which they rely predominantly on the resources of the survival self, varies. In the examples I have given, the survival dynamics are driving the team behaviour. And as with individuals, the willingness to be part of learning reviews or reflective processes is often minimal, as the survival self does not have the resources for reflective enquiry or compassion.

The survival defence behaviours will be familiar to you from previous chapters, as will their functionality to keep the trauma feelings suppressed. The survival dynamics within the team will be those of perpetrator–victim with the associated survival attitudes of each.

Management may accuse staff of being uncooperative, dysfunctional and resistant, and become punitive. Staff may accuse management of being unavailable, lazy, incompetent, stupid, and also become punitive. The team members and their manager will become angry, critical, frustrated, rejecting, and avoiding. The gulf will grow and the paranoia/blame will intensify. Trust will be severely damaged.

Those whose survival self involves narcissism may use the chaos to promote themselves. Those for whom control is a survival strategy may cease being cooperative and become even more controlling of what they can control. It will be deeply disturbing for everyone involved.

There will, of course, be denial, illusion, avoidance, and much acting out of survival behaviour. Many will take up the victim survival attitudes of complaining without offering solutions and then swinging to perpetration or self-aggrandisement. Where serious errors have been made on the part of one or more team members, the denial, protection, and justification of the perpetrator survival attitudes will be evident: *'I/We didn't do anything to contribute to this.'*

I have also experienced a collective paranoia or illusion that what has occurred was 'engineered' by someone who wants to destroy the team, and that there is a hero/heroine waiting in the wings to save them. The danger for the coach is of wanting to be that hero and stepping into the entanglement.

The survival strategies of working harder, or work avoidance, of drinking more, not participating in meetings, not getting involved, and even unconsciously creating a situation that may result in suspension to 'escape', will all be present. The stress levels activated by the situation can cause problems for individuals, too, with lack of sleep, heightened anxiety, and stress-related illness. Some team members may even become too ill to continue at work.

In *Trauma and Organisations* (Hopper, 2012), three dynamics within traumatised teams are identified, all of which are survival responses to the environment. The first is scapegoating, a form of perpetration that involves picking on and blaming someone, usually someone 'different', for many of the problems being experienced. This serves to protect other members of the team from facing up to the complex truth of the situation they find themselves in, as to do so would be unbearable. It is extremely painful for the person scapegoated, particularly as they will be excluded from the subgroups that necessarily will come together. The scapegoat is often seen as non-communicative or overbearing, lacking in understanding and different. Whistle-blowers are similarly scapegoated in traumatising organisations. Their mental health, motivations, and competence are questioned in an attempt to deal with the problem and allow the denial to continue.

Individuals scapegoated may often take on the behaviour projected on to them in the first place. For example, a whistle-blower's behaviour might become unstable, because of the pressures put on them, bringing about the behaviour they had previously been accused of. Such a dynamic is referred to as 'role suction' (Hopper, 2012).

The other two team survival responses are similar to the swing in victim attitude from helplessness to grandiosity. In a traumatised team, the victim survival dynamics swing between *'looking out for myself'* and *'an illusion of oneness with the others'* (Hopper, 2012). In *'looking out for myself'*, individuals will display a lack of collective responsibility for the situation they find themselves in and for resolving the problem. They come together in small subgroups, speaking critically about those outside their clique: '*They never pull their weight*', '*They act as if they are superior to us.*' This leads to internal divisions, making it impossible to achieve full team agreement.

Identification with a subgroup leads the trauma feelings of abandonment, fear, vulnerability, and aloneness to be stimulated. This brings the swing to the illusory: '*We are all the same, we think the same, there are no divisions between us.*' Despite previously or privately voiced differences of views, in this defensive process there is a 'joint front', as if those differences don't really exist. This brings an illusion of togetherness and belonging, other than for the scapegoat, who remains separated.

This illusory defence dynamic can be used to deny that any differences exist, owing to the anxiety of having to deal with them. This same defence might be used to deny obvious differences in race, culture, background, and experience between team members. Team members may say, '*We are the same, there is no difference between us, when we come together we are all the same.*' This prevents the anxiety raised by the differences, however, by denying them the opportunity to use them to benefit the team's growth is lost.

I have had experience of these survival dynamics in the past, as a member of a group I now understand to have been traumatised. We demonstrated all three of these survival dynamics. I felt abandoned, misunderstood, confused, furious, frustrated, let down. I huddled with a few friends to complain about the others and those in charge, and joined in the scapegoating. I also experienced the 'we are together' dynamic, as we came together to blame the institution. I was in a victim survival attitude, entangled with the dynamics in the group and unable to deal with it from a place of healthy autonomy. Time moved us on but at considerable lasting cost.

Conditions that can traumatise a team

By the time a team is demonstrating these survival responses, it is likely that there is a history of events that has damaged the attachment, equanimity, and identity of the team. If your client is leading or part of such a team, it can be helpful to set out the timeline of events, including before your client joined the team, if within the last three years. This is because of the cumulative nature of events, which will help the client to think about a way out of the trauma. You can enquire about events team members consider significant in their history. These are the ones that still cause hurt to or upset members, which they remain angry or confused about, which felt like a major betrayal and which left them feeling helpless and abandoned. The team may include individuals whose behaviour disturbs the equilibrium of the team, or new members appointed to address the situation, which is experienced as threatening or undermining by the original team members.

Such events might include having had frequent changes to the leadership of the team, within a short time span, some of which may have been very sudden and shocking. This is destabilising, as each change requires new relationships to be forged and the new leader often has to 'catch up' with the work and ethos of the team. The frequent changing of management structures and personnel activates trauma feelings of loss and abandonment, and over time a disregard for/mistrust of any manager in the 'here and now' because *they won't be staying long*'. There is a break in attachment bonding within the containment function of management. With each management change, trust is diminished and hard to rebuild. It is like children being shuffled through a series of foster homes. When a placement ends, the child may be moved suddenly without explanation or a proper goodbye that recognises the importance of the fostering relationship. As a result, bonding becomes increasingly impossible and insecure attachment patterns are reinforced.

All team members carry their own internal splits, their own suppressed trauma feelings and survival dynamics. Team relationships echo those of our early family relationships with siblings, parents, and extended family members – uncles, aunts, grandparents, and so on. To prevent work teams descending into these unhealthy dynamics, structures and processes that provide containment are needed, along with consistent clarity around the primary task of the team. The concept of containment is one of 'holding' the team dynamics and relationships together through coherent and consistent direction, management systems, and reasonably predictable interaction. These help the team to come together more regularly and healthily, as each member's place within the system becomes clear and acknowledged, and there are opportunities to resolve issues with respect. The factors that destroy the sense of safe-enough attachment through containment, or which destroy the consistency of expectations, responses or processes, and/or that bring perpetrator–victim dynamics into the team, are those which produce the traumatised responses.

The nature of the work, as in health care, can give rise to unconscious feelings of a lack of safety. How the work is organised provides social defences which are survival strategies, and which help to suppress any anxiety and vulnerability. This has been well documented in health care and other settings (Hinshelwood and Skogstad, 2000). In many teams, therefore, survival strategies and hypervigilance are already in operation.

In adult education, learners often feel ashamed, vulnerable, and anxious, yet experience joy and excitement. They look to the tutorial staff to contain the difficult trauma feelings by how they relate to, and manage, the learning experience. If this containment is broken – for example, through the tutor(s) frequently being absent or the overt favouritism shown to a student, or in how students are selected to move through the programme – the sense of safety and attachment will be affected and the perpetrator–victim dynamic emerges. Students who are anxious can also perpetrate on the group, from their sense of victimhood. This pulls other students into entangled relationships, as the following example illustrates:

> '*I was in the learning group coming together for the week's residential, and as you know the tutors have been ill a lot and they were in and out*

during the week. One of the participants was very provocative from the beginning. She ignored two of the requests made by the tutors about how to use the shared space, and was always late for sessions when we came together. While this seems insignificant in some ways, it had a negative impact on us all and yet no one said anything.'

Team survival dynamics can also be provoked when there are rumours or fears of sackings or redundancies. In organisations in which I have worked, the rumour mill was at work long before any announcement, so the fears and anxieties had already been stimulated. Everyone is left to consider: *'Will it be me?'* When redundancies are announced, those not made redundant will be relieved but are also likely to feel some guilt in relation to the misfortune of their colleagues. Being a 'favoured child' is a mixed blessing when it comes to projections of envy of others. If people have deep fears about rejection and abandonment, the threat of redundancy may be re-traumatising.

In all these examples, it is easy to say, *'Gosh how dreadful!'* or *'I would never manage like that'* – but be careful. We can all manage blindly out of our survival self-dynamics, thinking, *'It is the only way, it has to be done, there isn't time to handle it any other way'* without accessing the help available. Be careful of judging others and becoming a perpetrator or engaging your own grandiosity: *'I would never . . .'*. We are all caught up in survival dynamics at times, especially when there is a lot at stake. Many of us have learnt about containment, safety, and trust in organisational teams and about group dynamics. This learning can be put under great pressure in entangled traumatised teams, as I showed earlier in this chapter.

While you might also say, in relation to traumatised team members, *'But these are intelligent grown-ups'*, you need to remember that at the level of the trauma self, none of us is. We are all vulnerable children, terrified of abandonment. Where the 'here and now' environment is such that there are significant echoes of the 'there and then', the trauma and survival selves are enlarged with access to the healthy self diminished.

The invitation to become entangled with such teams through team coaching, or one-to-one coaching, is very strong. For this reason, it is essential to monitor yourself closely, through reflective self-supervision, and get good regular supervision with a coaching peer or coaching supervisor whose role is to support your reflective practice. Watch out for your rescuer being stimulated, or your perpetrator erupting or falling into victim survival attitudes. The strength of the dynamics is also why it is important to be mindful about your contracting, both with the organisational sponsor and the client. Is the contract a healthy one or a survival one? Are you being asked to become the manager by association or to do something that is impossible through illusion or denial? Or to become the 'organisational consultant' who analyses, diagnoses, and recommends solutions to the 'problem' under the guise of coaching. What can you really offer? Do not become trapped into thinking you can do the impossible. Do what you can to relate through your health autonomy, learn to identify when you are not.

A coach will be asked to work with teams such as these on an infrequent basis and you might be caught out not realising the depth or nature of the problem until you are working with the team. Traumatised teams need the containment factors to be re-established, with consistent leadership, decision-making, and responses to team requests and behaviour. Once a team is in a traumatised state, the risk of things going wrong increases, which enhances the trauma biography. A 'settling down' approach from management is needed, which allows the team members to regain self-regulation and come back into non-survival relationship with each other. They need to feel heard and respected. Leadership is required to make this happen, with insight and understanding. Team coaches will find it very difficult on their own. Coaching the leadership or involving a specialist consultancy may be more successful. Such teams do, however, need emotional and coaching support and one-to-one counselling or coaching may be valuable.

If you have agreed a one-to-one coaching contract, ensure you maintain the boundaries of that contract in terms of the focus and approach being used. The aim is to coach the healthy self from your healthy self. Where clients are entangled with their team, they may insist on meeting in their office. Traumatised clients may ask to meet in their home if they feel too unsafe at work to talk. In both cases, think very carefully about boundaries and what your response should be. I encourage you always to find a neutral space to work in and not to accept any invitation to become entangled.

Encourage clients who are part of traumatised teams to take their self-care seriously. Help them to identify what is healthy for them so they can step out of a victim survivor attitude and take full responsibility for what they are able to. Help them beware of entanglements, making the link with the 'there and then' and the 'here and now'. If they are feeling emotional distress, support them in thinking through what would be helpful for them, which might be short-term counselling or longer-term psychotherapy working with the trauma feelings.

7 Boundaries, challenges, and healing

When working with traumatised clients, we need to respect boundaries and promote clients' autonomy. We also need to be aware of how our trauma is activated in our work. In this chapter, I look at the boundary issues that might arise when working with clients who are more dominated by their survival self, including those with symptoms of mental illness, and what moving out of our trauma biography involves. I also talk about the importance of self-reflective practice and coaching supervision as a means of engaging with our own behaviour with clients.

Boundaries

People who are traumatised have had their boundaries and autonomy breached and it is important that we don't contribute to that being repeated. They are also less able to use the resources of their autonomy and protect their own boundaries. We need, therefore, to respect clients' autonomy and create safety through establishing and maintaining appropriate boundaries for the work.

The boundary to the work starts with the contracting process and how a coach describes the coaching they offer and what this means for clients. If the contracting includes talking about personal enquiry, using autobiography as information for the 'here and now' explorations, using body felt experience – both that of the coach and the client – there is clarity around the self-reflective process being part of coaching. If the client hasn't signed up for that, then the coach needs to be respectful of entering such territory. If it is not in the contract, it raises a question about what the nature of the work is. However, it might be, for example, that the coaching is internal to the organisation, colleague to colleague, where personal enquiry may not be an appropriate element of the contract. You can ask permission to enter this territory in any session, but your client must have the opportunity to refuse.

Even if clients have signed up to a self-explorative element to the coaching, as the coaching progresses the predominance of their survival self may inhibit that exploration, as the following coach describes:

> 'It just doesn't feel to me like real coaching, it feels very superficial. He won't engage with any self-enquiry and seems to have no interest in self-learning. I find it boring and feel I am not doing a good job.'

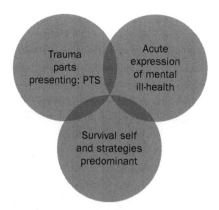

Figure 7.1 The three presentations

This can be frustrating for coaches whose favoured approach involves personal enquiry. The responses from clients activate their psyche-emotional needs for recognition, of being valued, feeling competent, and other survival needs. If we can avoid these responses within ourselves, we can continue to offer something of value.

Our contribution to the healing of trauma starts with our ability to create a safe space and to be fully present in our healthy self, listening attentively to all that is said or not said. Never underestimate the value to an individual of being listened to attentively, without being judged. Even when questions addressed to the healthy self of the client seem to be answered by the survival self, the question is not wasted, as it triggers some possibility for the healthy self to become active.

Before talking more about how trauma can be healed, let's consider what might be happening for clients where the coaching doesn't go so well or is challenging. Working with such clients makes us vulnerable to our own survival responses, including entanglement. When that happens, we stop using coaching approaches and techniques with the client, and become directive, avoidant, insecure in our practice or seek to rescue.

There are three broad areas that are a significant challenge to coaches, as they carry the potential for entanglement: trauma parts presenting, acute expression of mental ill health, and survival self and strategies predominate (see Figure 7.1).

Trauma parts presenting

The most likely presentation of the trauma parts is that of post-traumatic stress, with the client reporting sleeplessness, agitation, restlessness, ruminations on what has happened, terror nightmares, and flashbacks. The client may additionally describe becoming very angry and possibly violent in response to something that others might consider trivial. I have earlier given guidance about being with clients who are experiencing a re-traumatisation in the room becoming dissociated or cold, shaky, and distressed.

If you are concerned that clients might be suffering from post-traumatic stress, share that concern with them, enquire whether they have seen their general practitioner and whether they are having any therapy, and help them think through what action might be helpful and supportive for them. If clients wish to continue with the coaching, help them to be clear what they want from the sessions with you. Only continue with the coaching if you feel competent to do so.

The term 'normalisation' is used to refer to an intervention that aims to help clients understand that these responses to traumatising events are 'normal', that while they are deeply distressing and difficult, they are the kinds of responses that people have to such frightening or disturbing events. On top of the responses, many carry a thought that '*I shouldn't be feeling like this*', or '*that I should be over it all by now*', or '*the event wasn't that bad [when in fact it was], so why am I like this?*' Normalisation, therefore, is the way in which we can say: '*It is entirely understandable that you feel like this, in response to what you have experienced*', or '*When listening to you, what you have experienced sounds like a major event to me, so it is entirely understandable . . .*'. We can help take away some of the secondary stress that accumulates.

Acute presentation of mental ill health

Practitioners in the field of trauma therapy consider childhood trauma to underlie many expressions of mental ill health. A diagnosis of mental illness is not necessarily a barrier to effective coaching. It is helpful to ascertain if the client, whether a coaching or supervision client, has been treated or is being treated for a mental illness in the same way that it is helpful to know whether a client has been treated or is being treated for a physical illness.

When working with clients with long-term problems, it is helpful to develop a way to assess, at each session, whether their symptoms are such that coaching, or supervision, is unlikely to be useful. This might involve a scaling system, to identify how florid the symptoms are and having an agreement between the two of you about what is appropriate at different levels of the scale. This can be developed in association with clients, so their autonomy is respected.

With clients for whom it is a new problem, you can similarly discuss with them how best to respond to what they are experiencing. You can explore how coaching might be helpful and reality test that with them. They may, for example, find it helpful to explore what help they need and what healthy routines may be valuable to them. You can ask, '*What do you need?*' and '*What would be healthy for you?*' You can use scaling questions again, about levels of motivation and confidence in obtaining the help they think they need. High levels of motivation alone are not enough to support behaviour change, as the following example shows:

> 'My client scored 9/10 on motivation but then 4/10 on confidence. When I explored this with him, it was clear that the problem he faced was where to find the help he needed. He wasn't confident he would be able to do so.'

This facilitates a conversation about what would help him raise his confidence to 7/10 or more.

In their book *Coaching for Health* (2016), Rogers and Maini describe and illustrate a range of coaching approaches that support clients with mental or physical ill health take healthy action for themselves. People who are ill for a long time, or carers of those who are ill, often become socially isolated and lonely, it can be hard to gain the confidence to make contact with others.

It is natural to become concerned for clients whose symptoms are very present and distressing for them, as this coach illustrates:

> 'My client of 4 months has a history of depression and anxiety and I find I am very concerned for him. I am pleased he has now seen his doctor and is signed off sick. He says he doesn't really have any friends though and we have a session booked for next week and he has asked if we can still meet. He has been on the phone to me several times, and I am happy to take his call but not sure about going ahead with the session.'

The coach here was tempted to meet, as he felt he wanted to support the client. In such a situation, we need to check with ourselves about our desire to rescue. Is this coach taking more phone calls and getting more involved with his client's life than he would with other clients? And if so, what is driving that? Most coaches will be open to contact between sessions, and most clients respect the boundaries of that contact. However, those who are operating from survival may be unable to do that and our rescuing responses may draw us into a relationship that is no longer around coaching. If the sponsor of the coaching is supportive of the session going ahead, as the client is off sick, the coach can meet and talk with the client about how available he is for coaching, and if not, what other help he needs.

In some cases, clients who are experiencing mental ill health symptoms say they are not interested in contacting their doctor or anyone else, as in this illustration:

> 'I am really worried about my client. I have seen her a few times but yesterday she became very chaotic, dissociated, and started talking rapidly. I felt concerned for her mental health and asked her what was going on. I asked if she had been to her GP. She said she had seen the doctor in the past who had prescribed medication but that she had stopped taking it.

We talked about that and the option of going back to the GP. I asked her
if she had talked to those close to her, such as friends or family? She said
she hadn't. I tried to encourage her to think about what would be healthy
for her but it was hard for her to do that.'

Such acute expressions raise issues to do with duty of care, ethics, and confidentiality. In this case, the coach enquired about the client seeing the doctor and expressed concern about her. On reflection, there may be some learning to be had about what was avoided or that could have been done. However, the coach cannot rescue the client from her disturbed state. If the coach has listened attentively, and stayed in a healthy space herself, it is possible that this will have had a positive impact on the client, who may then go on to act for herself.

What do you do if your assessment is that a client is at risk, that they show no motivation for getting help from the doctor and they say to you, '*You can't tell anyone about this*' or '*Don't tell my boss/human resources*'? The following example, told by a supervisor, illustrates this:

'*Clare, the coach, was very concerned about Suri, her client. She asked*
for "emergency supervision", which I was happy to do as it is part of
my supervision contract. Suri had confided to Clare, during the session,
that she had been self-harming, cutting herself in places no one would
see. She said she couldn't go to the doctor as she was afraid of being hos-
pitalised. She also said she wasn't sleeping much and had no appetite.
The coaching had started several months earlier, and up until the last
month she had been very effective at work. Clare asked who else knew.
Suri's response was no one did, she wasn't in a relationship now, and
had withdrawn from her friends. Suri asked Clare to tell no one.'

What to do? It depends on what your contract is with the client. Some coaches, and most therapists, as part of contracting discuss circumstances in which they might feel the need to break client confidentiality and to whom. Examples of such situations include when a client shares their part in, or knowledge of, illegal activity, or the coach has serious concerns about the safety of the client, or of danger to others. This might be expressed as: '*Confidentiality is to be protected in all cir-*
cumstances other than when information is shared of criminal activity or if you
or others seem to be in danger. In any of these situations, I will always discuss
my thoughts and proposed actions with you.' It is good practice to talk with the client before you act, as the preferred outcome would be that the client acts on their own behalf. If you have had such a discussion with the client, whether captured in a written contract or not, you have the option to act and break the confidence the client has asked for by telling the person you identified to them. In talking it through, it may be that the client decides to disclose what is happening to them with an appropriate person. If you have an agreement with an organisational

sponsor, which the client knows about, it might be that you raise your concerns with the sponsor. However, this needs to be made clear from the start.

If you don't have a contracting agreement about confidentiality, you can work with the client to find an option that is acceptable to them in terms of getting professional help. For example, the client might decide to talk to a friend and ask her to go to the doctor with her.

If you take on a client who you know experiences periods of mental instability, it would be useful to talk with them at the outset about how to handle the illness if it becomes worse and who is to be told. The best option is for the client to consult their doctor, as that is where any risk can be evaluated. If the coach tells the doctor, it is likely that the doctor will wait for the client to make contact before acting, unless the client is known to them as being at risk.

We have a duty of care, within the boundaries of our coaching, and we always have an option to break the confidentiality we have with a client. It is important this is discussed with the client beforehand, and you explain what you are going to do and why, and that it is for the client's safety. Make sure it is for their safety though, and not you rescuing to make yourself feel better. If you break a confidence, this will have an impact on your relationship with the client, as it might be experienced as a breach of trust. It may result in a breakdown in the trust the client can consequently put in others. Traumatised people find it very hard to trust people in positions of influence over them, for obvious reasons. Have a conversation with your coaching supervisor about your concerns and the action you think is required. Breaking confidence is sometimes a risk worth taking but do so after much consideration.

Suicide

It might be that you have clients who say, '*I just can't go on*', or '*I think it would be better for all if I just disappeared*', or '*life just feels meaningless*', or express other suicidal thoughts. What is the right thing to do? First, keep listening, keep calm, and enquire what they mean. Be supportive not dismissive, remain open to what they are saying and don't close the conversation down. You can ask them directly if they are contemplating killing themselves and, if so, how? This helps clarify what they are saying and to identify the means available to them. Thank them for telling you and express empathy, such as '*I'm sad to hear you are hurting like this.*' If they have specific ideas about how to end their life, this is a high-risk situation. There is a lot online about how to end one's life, and it could be the client has already undertaken internet searches. You can also enquire if they have attempted to kill themselves before, or felt like it, and what happened? If they have tried before, this also indicates a high risk of them acting again. There are all kinds of myths about suicide, including that talking about it makes it more likely or that attempts are cries for help. Suicidal feelings need to be taken seriously, as they are an indicator of deep distress.

You can coach the healthy self about finding and getting appropriate help and support. Maintaining a client's confidence and abiding by their request not to tell someone may have to be broken for the safety of the client. This is why it is important to have had a contacting discussion about this possibility. Taking action may end the coaching relationship but you are not a clinician, you cannot assess the level of risk to such a client. There are some secrets we shouldn't hold. Get the support you need from your coaching supervisor as soon as is possible after such a conversation.

Suicide is a trauma survival strategy; the survival self wants to kill off the whole person to gain release from the emotional pain experienced and the attempts to keep it suppressed. It usually follows a period of emotional instability that is not always obvious to others. We may not be aware of the risk factors to the client, and they may not have shared their thoughts about taking their own life. Risk factors include a history of depression and other mental disorders, feelings of helplessness, previous suicide attempts, thoughts about how to end their life, an unwillingness to seek help, a family history of suicide, a history of alcohol or substance misuse, loss including significant financial or work-related loss, or being investigated for a serious error or misjudgement.

You may discover that a client you worked with in the past has taken their own life, which you no doubt will find very upsetting. Get support. You may wish to go back through your records and discuss it with your coaching supervisor, in the spirit of learning about signs, risk factors, and actions that might have been missed. It is important, however, not to take on a sense of misplaced responsibility for the client's actions and to avoid getting caught up in wanting to know why.

Survival self and strategies predominate

The third category involves individuals whose survival parts and strategies are the only or main way in which they engage with the world – that is, they are deeply entrenched defence systems. Such systems may reject help or involve a self-belief that the person does not need coaching or therapy at all, for example where a narcissistic survival dynamic is present.

It is helpful if you can make some assessment about the client's openness to coaching as a process. In the spirit of cooperation, we should always explore our observations with the client so that they can engage with them if they wish.

The survival self is not interested in personal growth or change. Its function is to protect the status quo, to support denial and illusion, and to keep the trauma feelings deeply buried. Where the survival self is the predominant way in which a client relates to the world, there is a very limited capacity for accessing the heathy self.

Figure 7.2 illustrates the splits in the psyche when the survival self is predominant. If clients with this internal dynamic come into coaching, it is likely to be as a result of a major problem at work. Otherwise, stepping into a relationship such as coaching, which is a relatively intimate meeting between two people, feels too threatening. While the healthy self is there, the survival and trauma selves are enlarged, with associated high levels of stress, which could be seen as being normal to the client.

People with the psyche structure shown in Figure 7.3 primarily use the resources in their survival self to manage their life. However, they have access

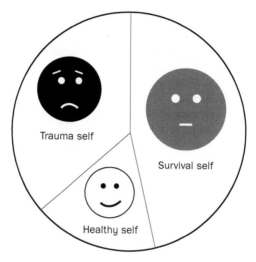

Figure 7.2 Predominantly survival self

Source: Adapted from Vivian Broughton (2014).

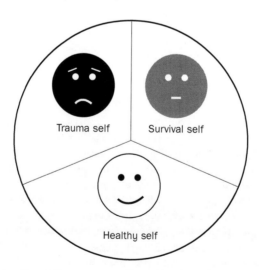

Figure 7.3 More healthy self

Source: Adapted from Vivian Broughton (2014).

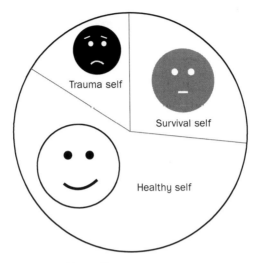

Figure 7.4 Predominantly healthy self

Source: Adapted from Vivian Broughton (2014).

to their healthy self. The trauma self is also activated, with associated levels of stress. How they are in life will depend on whether they have learnt how to access and trust their healthy self. We will meet such traumatised people in coaching.

In Figure 7.4, there is access to the healthy self and its resources necessary for self-reflection and knowing what is wanted and healthy. The survival self is present and may be propelled into the driving position if the environment is experienced as hostile. The trauma self is not highly activated so stress levels will be within the normal range.

While I have illustrated three possible scenarios, there are of course many others in between. A big challenge for anyone who carries trauma, even if they can access their healthy self-resources, is whether they can trust what the healthy self tells them. Accessing it is one thing, trusting it is another.

There are some indicators that can help us assess the level of access to the healthy self:

The capacity for compassionate self-reflection and self-enquiry.	You will discern this in the way clients talk about themselves and others. You will experience their capacity for self-reflection in response to powerful questions you ask.

The capacity for self-regulation and self-control.	It's easy to become stressed by events. That is a normal healthy response. However, if we have a limited capacity for self-regulation, and already suffer from toxic stress levels, we are pushed into survival responses. How stressed does the client feel most of the time? If stress is an issue, have they found techniques that help them? Are they willing to put the time in and the discipline needed to bring stress levels down? A marker of the healthy self is that they are willing, and that they see it as a priority.
The presence of the persecutor–victim dynamics and survival attitudes.	Are clients able to take responsibility for their choices and actions? Do you meet their persecutor in the coaching room, albeit subtly? Are they presenting victim or perpetrator survival attitudes?

You will also gain a sense of the survival self and strategies through your relationship with clients and what you observe about their behaviour. How do they relate to you, do they push you away or pull you towards them seeking dependency? Do they want more of your time by phoning or emailing between sessions, or asking you to read things they send you? How about the stories they tell about relationships at work? What are their beliefs about relating to and trusting others?

Where the healthy self is relating to us, we feel a connection with the client. There is good eye contact, relaxed body language, and openness to possibility, together with the capacity for voicing what is needed. The client can say what they want and what is healthy for them. However, where a client's survival self is relating to us, we may feel controlled by them, or the client may intellectualise, over-analyse, use challenge or humour, all ways of deflecting from you. You are likely to meet denial, illusion, and addiction in some form, most commonly to work or exercise. You will also meet the perpetrator–victim dynamics. Applying these elements to the three structures described earlier provides a way of helping us to understand the dynamics and how to respond.

When the survival self is predominant as the core way of functioning, there will be a low capacity or desire for self-enquiry; there will be rigidity in thinking about possibilities with a lot of 'I can't', 'I must', 'I have to', and 'you don't understand' statements. Your relationship with the client will feel challenging and rejecting. There will be evidence of perpetrator–victim dynamics in their work lives and you might feel these in your relationship with them. You will observe a range of survival strategies and the survival or adaptive self in their narrative. The individual may have been very successful in their career but there may be signs that this is no longer sustainable, for example, being passed over for promotion or failing significantly for the first time. Exhaustion is likely, or certainly 'running on empty'; draining whatever energy is available to keep surviving. They might show signs of being on the verge of burnout but deny it and be 'too busy' to come to sessions or come late and leave early.

Here are some examples of coaches who are in their survival self in relationship with such clients:

> 'I find him so hard to be with. He is rather patronising and questions my qualifications; he also blocks me if I try to open things up for exploration. He is quite fidgety, always has his phone on and checks it through the session. I find him rather narcissistic and I know I shouldn't say this, but I don't really like him, and I don't like how he talks about his staff. He can be very charming but . . . I realised I had just semi-switched off, just waiting for the time to be over, and letting him direct the process and I really hope that he might say he wants to end the coaching. He can't make the next session, and now we are trying to rearrange it.'

> 'I find her very difficult. She is very abrasive and dismissive of any of my interventions. I found myself using all kinds of tools and exercises to try to get her engaged but nothing seemed to work. I felt she really disliked me or thinks I am stupid. She is very clever and uses her thinking in quite an attacking way. I could feel myself shrivel up. I must be doing something wrong but feel I have tried everything.'

You may find such clients extremely challenging. The invitation to become entangled is powerful and nearly always responded to. Get supervision early to help you stay in your healthy self and relate with healthy autonomy. Do whatever you can to aim your coaching to the healthy self, but don't expect a healthy response. And don't be surprised if a client hasn't attended to actions agreed upon at the end of the previous session. Let go of your need to be successful or to get an outcome. Listen attentively, enquire how they are experiencing coaching. If relevant, raise the issue of therapy, but don't expect a positive response. If you feel the coaching is stalled, talk it through with the client and explore what is possible.

When there is more healthy self available to clients (see Figure 7.3), the survival self is still predominant. Be aware of the risks of becoming entangled and do what you can to stay in your healthy self. You will experience the client's survival strategies and self, of which the perpetrator–victim dynamics will be a part. Psychoeducation may be useful, using the split in the psyche model (Ruppert, 2014), together with other models and tools that aid self-awareness about trauma dynamics. Be wary of coaching the survival self to work even harder and longer or to do more of what it is already doing. The trauma feelings may break through, with the client expressing distress and a sense of helplessness.

The following example is of a client, told by a coach, who has more of his healthy self available, as seen in his response to the model, but who is still dominated by his survival self:

> 'David is a strange mixture, at times I find him very defensive and hostile, taking control of the process and almost pushing me out; I realise I go silent and then I start talking a lot. It feels we go nowhere. And then there is a moment where something shifts, like when I showed him the model and talked it through. He seemed to soften a bit and I felt a different engagement. We talked about what might be happening and what may be helpful for him in terms of actions he could instigate. But then it seemed to close over and I was back in the "tennis match"; and yes I do feel competitive when that happens. I find it difficult not to join him in the intellectual discussions, and enjoy them but realise then that we are off course. He doesn't really look at me either; I think he finds it easier when we are looking at something together, like the model. He says he is not sure what he is getting from the coaching, which I find hard.'

The 'easiest' configuration to work with in coaching is that when the healthy self is uppermost (see Figure 7.4). There is enough healthy self, self-compassion, capacity for empathy, emotional intelligence, and contact with the body/gut feeling within clients, which they can also trust. It is possible that the relative size of each self alters in response to a change in the environment, with the survival self becoming more prominent as the trauma self is stimulated. However, there is a memory of a healthy self 'being' that clients can draw on and use to resolve or develop issues in their lives now, as in the following example:

> 'Jay feels easy to be with. He is focused and clear on what he wants; he is interested in my feedback and observations, that is not to say he takes them on blindly but engages with them. He recognises his stressors and has developed some ways to regulate them, he goes running but not obsessively. He has what seems to me, to be a realistic assessment of his talents and opportunities; also recognises where his developmental possibilities are. He is really enjoying most of the work he is involved with but recognises it is almost time to move on and feels okay about that once he has the right option. I feel we are working well together and he is making the changes happen that he wants.'

Figure 7.5 illustrates how the predominance of the survival self and healthy self changes across the spectrum, making links to the extent of the trauma biography and to the likely impact on the coach.

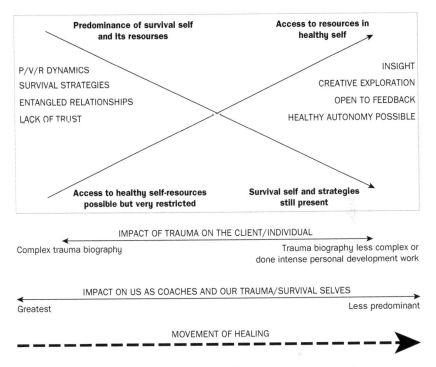

Figure 7.5 Summary of survival self-presentation

Moving out of trauma

It is possible to move out of the trauma dynamics from the splits in the psyche. This requires a commitment to and investment of time in accessing a therapeutic process. This may be painful, as moving out of trauma requires us to experience the deep suppressed trauma feelings in a safe way, face the truth of our experience, and bring the survival self into conscious awareness. The alternative, doing nothing, will result in continued perpetration and victimhood, repeated entanglements, lack of self-compassion, and deep unhappiness. Traumatised people are traumatising parents, managers, and team members, and the cycle will continue.

Lasting healing requires engagement with the trauma self, which is not the territory of coaching. However, coaching can support trauma healing through the identification of elements of the survival self, strategies and dynamics, and using the healthy self to limit access to re-traumatising environments.

In support of clients' intentions for their coaching, you can help them make links to the 'there and then' to understand something about their trauma. You do this through your own enhanced understanding and by using the qualities, skills, and process interventions that are a part of coaching. You can only be effective in this if you have facilitated a sense of safety in the client. I have already talked of boundaries and issues to do with confidentiality, components of creating safety. The sense of safety, and trust in you, is also facilitated through consistency of your responses, achieved through you not becoming entangled or using your survival strategies.

The coaching qualities needed include:

Having self-awareness and capacity for self-exploration	Having the capacity for self-regulation
Being able to be present and attuned to the client; listening attentively	Having good contact with the body and the felt experience
Being non-judgemental and curious	Having empathy and compassion

The coaching skills required include the appropriate use of powerful questions, such as, *'what do you want?'*, *'what do you need?'*, and *'what would be healthy for you?'* Effective coaching uses observation, feedback, acknowledgement, and the timely selection and use of tools to aid self-awareness and understanding. You can use the trauma biography in ways to connect experience in the 'there and then' with the 'here and now' and in challenging survival self-narratives. You need to give clients space to talk about distressing memories and feelings and to bring the felt experience into awareness. You will, by now, recognise that these are all elements of healthy autonomy. Your main task is to stay in your own healthy self. From this space, you can help clients be clear about what they want from coaching and from you.

You can help educate clients about trauma and survival through introducing, with their permission, the split in the psyche model (Ruppert, 2012) to illustrate behaviour you have observed in them. In introducing information such as this, there may be a concern about 'making it worse by mentioning trauma'. If you introduce the model uncompassionately, without emphasising the benefits in the past of the survival self or the existence of the healthy self, or are entangled in rescuer mode or as persecutor, you may indeed make it worse in the 'here and now'. However, 'there and then' can't be made any worse than it already is.

It is the when and how of introducing the ideas of the traumatised psyche and the survival self that is crucial. When handled appropriately, as when introducing any concept or tool, clients recognise the metaphor and can relate it to themselves. You do not need to go into their trauma history as the survival strategies demonstrate the underlying trauma. Sometimes, the model prompts clients to share something relevant from their past and to make the connection with the present. For many, it will be the first time they have linked their experience from the past to the present:

> *'That is so helpful. I have never before made the connection with my experience as a child with an alcoholic abusive father and vulnerable*

mother to how I am dealing with this huge project now. I can see that I tried to rescue my father so that he wouldn't be abusive to my mother; and that I am still rescuing in the hope that I will be valued. To have put those together is very powerful for me.'

You can explain that the 'there and then' can become confused with the 'here and now'. That as children we had no options open to us but now, as adults, we have different choices available to us, we have more internal resources to respond to the environment. You can also help clients separate the past from the present and gain self-awareness:

> *'I recognise that I tend either to rescue men or to see them as perpetrators. I hadn't connected that to my father, but I can see I am replaying the patterns from the past in how I am responding to my male bosses.'*

> *'It had never occurred to me that my fear of putting myself out there related to how my mother never thought I was good enough, nor encouraged my efforts, and tried to make me a different person. I know she was in a very difficult situation herself and have always thought it was something I should have grown out of. But I get that it is still there and operating in the here and now.'*

If you find yourself intellectualising in relation to theory, or as part of self-aggrandisement or control, however subtle, you are in your survival self.

You can help clients recognise their survival strategies for what they are and gradually identify what triggers them in the 'here and now'. This can lead to an exploration of how to manage stress and anxiety levels, so that clients can slow down the 'stimulus–response' dynamic and perhaps respond differently. You can also talk about the survival self, its identifications and the narratives we been given or constructed, and about entangled relationships. You can help clients recognise that access to the healthy self is generally helped by slowing down. This might be just pausing more to take stock and might also include the introduction of mindfulness or meditation practice, having time to 'be with oneself' in a way that feels healthy. This is part of the *'what would be healthy for you?'* question.

Some people think that the purpose of trauma healing is forgiveness and reconciliation. That is not so. The idea of forgiveness can be a survival illusion, if it denies the pain and suffering caused and is a form of survival attachment from a trauma of love. Freeing ourselves from entanglements with perpetrators requires us to engage with our feelings of being their victim, and the impact it has had on us; we can then face our own truth, from our felt experience. We can state they did us harm and go on to recognise that they too were traumatised, but we do not need to rescue them from that fate. If we remain angry and want revenge, we remain entangled with them.

You can suggest that therapy may be helpful, where appropriate, so that the client can access specialist help. The client may be having therapy alongside coaching, in which case you need to be clear about boundaries and check with the client about how coaching can best fit with that other work. It shouldn't mean that you do not bring self-enquiry into the coaching, but that the client will take some of what arises in coaching into therapy and vice versa. The emphasis of the two practices is different but complementary.

I have mentioned several times the need to consult your supervisor whenever you have a client whom you experience as challenging, or when you realise you are in an entanglement with the client or the sponsoring organisation. Sometimes your own self-reflective practices will be enough, but it is one of the functions of supervision to keep us, as far as is possible, coaching from our healthy self, protecting the client and the coach.

Coaching supervision involves exploring the client work, side by side with the coach. It is a process of self-enquiry and reflection about what was going on for the coach, what impact the environment had, and what is being presented through the client's behaviour. It is an action-learning process, not about correction or judgement. At times, supervision can be therapeutic in the same way that coaching can be.

Understanding this trauma model and theory, and the impact on clients and coaches, can improve supervision, in the same way it improves coaching. Coaching supervisors need to be aware of their own trauma survival dynamics and how they may become entangled with their clients. They, too, need to keep relating from their healthy autonomy.

One of my primary messages throughout has been that as long as we stay coaching from our healthy self, using the coaching qualities, skills, and techniques we have, with an awareness of trauma, that's all we need when working with clients who are traumatised. The problems arise when we become entangled with the client. Many coaches are traumatised from their own trauma biographies. We carry our own survival self-identity, strategies, behaviour, and dynamics. Most of us are not operating in healthy autonomy all or most of the time. The question is, '*are we able to do so often enough?*' and, if not, '*how can we do it more often?*'

The ways in which we can help ourselves are the same as those we use with our clients. Practise listening to your healthy voice, the part of you that knows what is true and grounded. This might need you to slow down, to sit with things, rather than rush to action. Mediation and mindfulness help with this, as does using reflective writing or similar writing about your client work on a daily basis. Such writing, as for all action learning, involves exploring what was happening for you, what you noticed about your inner experience, what you noticed about your 'doing' and your interaction with the client. The aim is to begin to track your survival self and strategies and to map out your patterns and what the triggers are. We need to be kind and compassionate towards ourselves when we realise we have been in survival with our clients. Use it as data, valuable information to be explored in your reflective enquiry.

Find a colleague who has also read this book, is familiar with the concepts or has been on workshops with you to talk through what you are noticing about yourself in your client work, and what you are learning about the dynamics using a trauma theory lens. Find other ways to develop your learning and understanding about working effectively with clients who want to change their survival responses to trauma. There are many such workshops available. Choose carefully, but as was once said to me, '*You can't not learn something useful if you remain open to the teaching.*' Be curious how your survival strategies appear as a learner, for example, do you feel envy and stop listening, feel argumentative or bored, or recognise self-aggrandisement?

It is important to take your own trauma seriously. This means doing your own work and not trying to sort out other people's trauma as a way of avoiding dealing with your own. Taking it seriously isn't about blaming others, it is about engaging with a deep process of self-development and taking self-responsibility for your choices in the 'here and now'. If you wish to do therapeutic work to help yourself, there are therapists who understand and work with trauma. Do your research about what is available and what you feel drawn to. Take advice and ensure there is a solid grounding behind the practice and practitioner.

Summary

The following is a summary of the coaching skills and interventions that are needed to support trauma healing and effective coaching around the survival self.

- Create a safe space by establishing and maintaining appropriate boundaries for the coaching.
- In the coaching contract, include self-reflection, somatic exploration, and autobiography as elements of the coaching process, if you are competent to use these techniques. Be mindful in the contracting about how you want to handle breaking confidentiality should you feel duty of care demands it.
- Be fully present, with attuned listening. Be aware of your body and the information it can give you. Listen to the spoken, implied, and body communication.
- Always ask for and obtain permission from the client for using the split in the psyche model (Ruppert, 2012), the survival victim attitudes and others. Ensure you fully understand them before using them. Use them in your own self-reflection before introducing them to clients.
- If introducing the split in the psyche model, emphasise the healthy self and its resources. Link the survival self and strategies to what the client has shared with you or you have observed.
- Use the autobiography to bring awareness to childhood narrative and experience. The narrative is open to challenge and exploration, with the client's permission. The experience, however, should be validated, as should emotions.

- Offer clients observations about the potential 'there and then' in the 'here and now'; ensure it is possible for them to reject your observation if they choose.
- Listen out for survival self-language: *'should/must/have to'*.
- Bring clients' body/felt experience into their awareness if that feels appropriate.
- Heighten your awareness of illusion, denial and distraction, and how they appear in the client's narrative and your own. Develop skills to offer challenge to such survival strategies.
- Heighten your awareness of perpetrator and victim dynamics, including the survival attitudes of both perpetrators and victims. Become tuned into your own survival attitudes and perpetrations on self or others.
- Recognise entanglements, both your own and those of your clients. If clients wish to explore these dynamics, help them understand what is going on for them.
- Thank clients who disclose troubling experience or emotions for entrusting you with their story. Validate and acknowledge these disclosures.
- At all times, stay coaching. Do not become a faux-therapist or counsellor. Stay within the boundaries of your competence. Seek supervision if you believe you are caught up in an entanglement.
- Staying coaching means demonstrating the coaching qualities, skills, and techniques of effective coaching. Put aside any survival needs to be successful, or impressive, or right. Stay present in the 'here and now', in your healthy autonomy.
- Know and keep within the limitations of your competence. It isn't the function of coaching to work with the trauma self. Ensure you don't, as the risks of re-traumatisation are high. If clients are distressed, allow them to be without rescuing or reassuring.
- Do work on your own splits in the psyche with an appropriate practitioner, so that you deepen your own self-awareness and trauma healing.
- Have a coaching supervisor and use the supervisory process for your own self-enquiry about what happens to you with particular clients.
- Working round the survival self requires coaching experience and competence. Practitioners need to be unconsciously competent as coaches so that they can be present without thinking about what to do next.
- If coaches want to develop their effectiveness in working around the survival self, they should develop their coaching skills and presence. From that foundation, they need to widen the understanding of the trauma dynamics and how to respond in coaching. If coaches, early in their practice, feel they are highly motivated to work with people who are traumatised, my response is the same. I would also add 'watch out for the rescuer' being enacted.

Conclusion

This book can only be an introduction, the start of a learning process in this area or a continuation of one. Words can tell us so much but getting experiential body-based information can give us more. A large component of my learning in this field has been from doing experiential work on myself and contributing to the experiential trauma work of others. From that experience, I have built up my knowledge and understanding. I think I have participated in well over 500 pieces of trauma work using the identity-orientated psyche-trauma process of Professor Franz Ruppert, before that a hundred or so family systems constellations. I have read widely in the field, have worked therapeutically with clients one-to-one, and facilitated experiential work in groups. And, I have brought the understanding of my own trauma and survival responses into my coaching supervision and practice.

My teachers have been Franz Ruppert, Vivian Broughton, Alexandra Smith, and Gabor Maté. I have learnt a lot, too, from the writings of Bessel van der Kolk, Allan Schore, Irvin Yalom, Marian Woodman, Alice Miller, and Babette Rothschild. Before them there was all the learning from the wider therapy world and of course from the thousands of hours coaching and coaching teaching I have done over the past twenty-five years. It has been a process of evolution.

I hope this will take you on to somewhere useful, stimulating, and healthy in your practice. If you have any responses to this book and what I am describing, please email your comments to me. I would be pleased to hear from you. My email address is jvs@anaptys.co.uk.

Bibliography

Ainsworth, M., Blehar, M., Waters, E. and Wall, S. (1979) *Patterns of Attachment: A psychological study of the strange situation.* Hillsdale, NJ: Lawrence Erlbaum Associates.

Axelrod, S.A. (1999) *Work and the Evolving Self: Theoretical and clinical considerations.* Hillsdale, NJ: The Analytic Press.

Babiak, P. (1995) When psychopaths go to work: a case study of an industrial psychopath, *Applied Psychology: An International Review*, 44 (2): 171–188.

Bowlby, J. (1953) *Childcare and the Growth of Love.* London: Penguin Books.

Bowlby, J. (1971) *Attachment and Loss*, Vol. 1. Harmondsworth: Penguin Books.

Bowlby, J. (1979) *The Making and Breaking of Affectional Bonds.* London: Tavistock Publications.

Broughton, V. (2014) *Becoming Your True Self*, 2nd edn. Steyning: Green Balloon Publishing.

Davis, D.M. (2018) *The Beautiful Cure Harnessing Your Body's Natural Defences.* London: The Bodley Head.

Freyd, J. (1996) *Betrayal Trauma: The logic of forgetting childhood abuse.* Cambridge, MA: Harvard University Press.

Garland, C. (ed.) (1998) *Understanding Trauma: A psychoanalytic approach*, 2nd edn. London: Karnac Books.

Gerhardt, S. (2004) *Why Love Matters: How affection shapes a baby's brain.* London: Brunner-Routledge.

Greenspan, M. (2004) *Healing Through the Dark Emotions: The wisdom of grief, fear, and despair.* London: Shambhala.

Hill, S. (2018) *Where Did You Learn to Behave Like That?* UK: Dialogix.

Hinshelwood, R.D. and Skogstad, W. (eds.) (2000) *Observing Organisations: Anxiety, defence and culture in health care.* London: Routledge.

Holmes, J. (2001) *The Search for the Secure Base: Attachment theory and psychotherapy.* Hove: Brunner-Routledge.

Hopper, E. (ed.) (2012) *Trauma and Organisations.* London: Karnac Books.

Horney, K. (1950) *Neurosis and Human Growth.* New York: Norton.

Kalsched, D. (1996) *The Inner World of Trauma.* London: Routledge.

Kalsched, D. (2013) *Trauma and the Soul.* London: Routledge.

Karpman, S. (2014) *A Game Free Life.* San Francisco, CA: Drama Triangle Publications [see www.KarpmanDramaTriangle.com].

Kets de Vries, M. (2006) *The Leader on the Couch.* Chichester: Wiley.

Kets de Vries, M., Korotov, K. and Florent-Treacy, E. (2007) *Coach and Couch. The psychology of making better leaders.* London: Palgrave Macmillan.

Levine, P.A. (1997) *Waking the Tiger: Healing trauma*. Berkeley, CA: North Atlantic Books.

Levine, P.A. (2015) *Trauma and Memory: Brain and body in a search for the living past*. Berkeley, CA: North Atlantic Books.

Maté, G. (2003) *When the Body Says No: Exploring the stress–disease connection*. New York: Wiley.

Maté, G. (2013) *In the Realm of the Hungry Ghosts: Close encounters with addiction*. Toronto: Vintage Canada.

McGarvey, D. (2017) *Poverty Safari*. Edinburgh: Luath Press.

McGilchrist, I. (2009) *The Master and his Emissary*. London: Yale University Press.

Miller, A. (2001) *The Truth Will Set You Free*. New York: Basic Books.

Ogden, P. and Fisher, J. (2013) *The Body as a Resource: A therapist's manual to sensorimotor psychotherapy*. London: Norton.

Ogden, P. and Fisher, J. (2015) *Sensorimotor Psychotherapy: Interventions for trauma and attachment*. London: Norton.

O'Sullivan, S. (2015) *It's All in Your Head: True stories of imaginary illness*. London: Chatto & Windus.

Proctor, B. (2008) *Group Supervision: A guide to creative practice*. London: SAGE.

Rogers, J. (2017) *And how's your mental health* [see http://www.coachingandtrauma.com/blog/].

Rogers, J. and Maini, A. (2016) *Coaching for Health: Why it works and how to do it*. London: Open University Press.

Rothschild, B. (2000) *The Body Remembers: The psychophysiology of trauma and trauma treatment*. London: Norton.

Ruppert, F. (2012) *Symbiosis and Autonomy* (trans. J. Stuebs and R. Hosburn, ed. V. Broughton). Steyning: Green Balloon Publishing.

Ruppert, F. (2014) *Trauma, Fear and Love* (ed. V. Broughton). Steyning: Green Balloon Publishing.

Ruppert, F. (2016) *Early Trauma: Pregnancy, birth and the first years of life* (trans. J. Stuebs and R. Hosburn, ed. V. Broughton). Steyning: Green Balloon Publishing.

Ruppert, F. and Banzhaf, H. (2018) *My Body, My Trauma, My I* (ed. V. Broughton). Steyning: Green Balloon Publishing.

Schore, A. (2001) The effect of early relational trauma on right brain development, affect regulation, and infant mental health, *Infant Mental Health Journal*, 22 (1/2): 201–269.

Schore, A. (2010) Relational trauma and the developing right brain: the neurobiology of broken attachment bonds, in T. Baradon (ed.) *Relational Trauma in Infancy* (pp. 19–47). London: Routledge.

Sieff, D.F. (2015) *Understanding and Healing Emotional Trauma*. London: Routledge.

Siegel, D. (2011) *Mindsight: Transform your brain with the new science of kindness*. Oxford: One World Publications.

Stern, D. (1998) *The Interpersonal World of the Infant*. London: Karnac Books.

van der Kolk, B. (2015) *The Body Keeps The Score:. The mind, brain and body in the transformation of trauma*. London: Allen Lane.

Whitworth, L., Kimsey-House, H. and Sandahl, P. (1998) *Co-Active Coaching: New skills for coaching people towards success in work and life.* Palo Alto, CA: Davis-Black Publishing.

Winnicott, D. (1964) *The Child, the Family and the Outside World.* London: Pelican Books.

Yalom, I. (2002) *The Gift of Therapy.* London Piatkus Books.

Index

Printed and bound by CPI Group (UK) Ltd, Croydon, CR0 4YY

23/01/2025

01824978-0005